P9-CDP-175

Paul Robeson, *Negro*

By

ESLANDA GOODE ROBESON

New York and London
HARPER & BROTHERS
mcmxxx

For Our Son

CONTENTS

PAUL ROBESON
Negro

I. THE NEGRO PREACHER

At the beginning of the twentieth century Princeton, New Jersey, although only about an hour from New York by train, was far removed from New York in other ways. After the freeing of the slaves in 1865, Negroes had very slowly migrated from the South to the North in search of work and wages. It happened that several Negroes from North Carolina settled in Princeton and the nearby towns of Westfield and Somerville, and formed the nucleus of a definite Negro community. When other Negroes from that section of the South decided to go North, they naturally got in touch with relatives and friends who had already undertaken the great adventure, and went to live with or near them. In the early nineteen-hundreds the Negro section in Princeton had all the earmarks of a Negro section in the South, with the sole important difference that the Negroes were now free; their new homes were somewhat better than the old log cabins; their children went to

1

school; instead of the revival meetings held in a tent they had a real church, in which they took great pleasure and pride. The Negroes themselves occupied more or less the same servile position to the whites, because most of them had entered into domestic service—that being the only work they knew.

In this community, and in similar communities all over the North, the church became an institution of tremendous importance. The hard-working Negroes saved their pennies for the collection plate on Sunday; the chu'ch was the bright spot of their existence; their "religion" became to a large extent their only physical, mental, and emotional outlet; the chu'ch was the social center. Here, after long hard days of toil in kitchens they could dream of the pearly gates of heaven and streets paved with gold, and of rest; after the week of being quiet and meek in the "big house," saying "yes'm" and "no'm," they could raise their voices and sing loudly Sunday mornings and evenings. These people who had so little time for fun and dancing rocked their bodies in abandon to the powerful rhythm of the spirituals; many a sister found the extraordinary rhythm too much for her nerves, and threw up her arms with a shout of "Hallelujah"

2

or "My Jesus," and sank down exhausted but strangely rested. And the sermons: just simple ones from Bible stories, usually with vivid word-pictures of hell fire and damnation for the wicked, and rest and peace and golden crowns for the righteous; these sermons were accepted literally by the congregation, who had so little play for their vivid imaginations. After a rousing sermon nearly all these poor hard-worked folk were entirely happy; they had gone to heaven and been welcomed as human beings by St. Peter; they had been led up to God's golden throne and been crowned by Him; the milk and honey of heaven was a welcome change from their monotonous diet of corn-pone and bacon, and the golden picture was a complete rest from their drab homes. From such an atmosphere came the spiritual "Sit Down": tired women who had been on their feet all week cooking, washing, scrubbing, came to church on Sunday and were told that heaven was a place where you *sat down,* and that God was a kind man who sort of shook hands in welcome and then invited you to sit down and rest a little while:

> I'm goin' up to heaven an' sit down,
> Goin' up to heaven an' sit down,

3

Oh, sit down, sister, sit down, child,
Sit down an' rest a little while.

I'll see my Lord, He'll say sit down,
See my Lord, He'll say sit down,
Oh, sit down, sister, sit down, child,
Sit down an' rest a little while.

Yo' back is bent from burdens borne,
There are furrows on yo' brow,
Oh, come, my child, you're welcome home,
Yo' troubles are over now;

Do sit down; sit down; sit down;
Yes, my Lord. Hummmmmmmmmm;
Hallelujah, wid my Jesus.

It is interesting to follow the growth of the Negro
Church. In the South after slavery, several small
Negro communities would jointly support a
preacher. This preacher travelled back and forth
from one place to another, holding services and ad-
ministering to his various congregations; in return
he received his board and lodging, his railroad
fare, his clothing, and occasionally a small amount
of money. The congregations maintained a meeting
hall of some kind where the services were held.
Gradually, as the congregations could afford it,

FOOTBALL

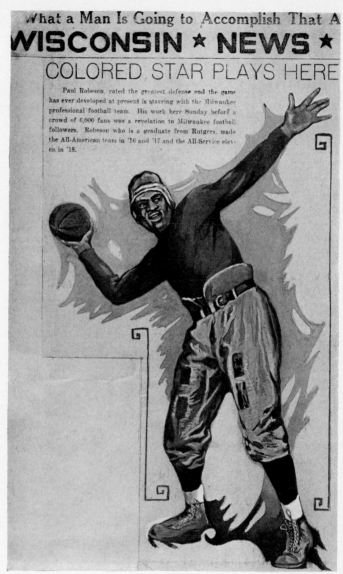

What a Man Is Going to Accomplish That A

WISCONSIN ★ NEWS ★

COLORED STAR PLAYS HERE

Paul Robeson, rated the greatest defense end the game has ever developed at present is starring with the Milwaukee professional football team. His work here Sunday before a crowd of 6,000 fans was a revelation to Milwaukee football followers. Robeson who is a graduate from Rutgers, made the All-American team in '16 and '17 and the All-Service eleven in '18.

FOOTBALL

THE BEGINNING OF THE FAMOUS "FORWARD PASS"

they secured the exclusive services of a preacher, and later on they built a proper church.

When the Negroes migrated to the North, they took their customs with them. The travelling preacher eventually found a "charge" that could maintain him. He at first lived at the home of the most prosperous parishioner, and held services in a hall. Nearly everyone else in the community worked hard, but the preacher was idle save on prayer-meeting nights and Sundays. This set him as a person apart from the rest. He usually filled his time by calling on the sick, and by making rounds of visits in the evenings, talking with the members of his flock, advising and encouraging them. He was usually a man of some education; he could read and write, and often was fairly well trained. This further marked him as a man apart from the rest. He read and wrote letters for his flock, counted for them, interpreted the fundamental laws for them. But, last and most important, he actually personified their religion to these literal-minded people, and religion was the great thing in their lives. God and the Church and the preacher were so closely associated in their simple minds that often any one of three meant all three to them. The preacher was worshipped on Sundays when he read and expounded the gospel; his flock admired and thoroughly enjoyed his oratory in the pulpit; they profoundly respected the education which enabled him to read and write and understand things. So gradually the preacher became the important and most necessary person, both spiritually and practically, in the community.

In return for all his efforts the congregation gave the preacher, or rather the Church, all the money it could possibly rake and scrape together; he was expected to have a good living out of this money, and the remainder was usually put toward a "fund." Invariably this fund was finally used to build an imposing church; first the basement of the church was built and the services were held there; once this definite beginning was accomplished, everyone grew anxious to finish the building properly. Socials were held, picnics, concerts, dinners, suppers, fairs; the members of the church fell to and supplied the food and entertainment for the least possible expense, and the people paid the highest fee they could afford to attend these functions. Naturally the fund grew rapidly, and as the church became the home not only of their religious life, but of their social life as well, it assumed a greater importance in the minds of the congrega-

6

tion. They built the rest of the church over the original basement; later on they built a parsonage next the church. As they grew richer they built more and more beautiful churches, installed organs; the minister was put on a really good salary, and was given an automobile instead of the original eggs, butter, sugar, and flour. From time to time there were great celebrations as the church emerged from under its heavy weight of debt; these celebrations are still held, and are known as "the burning of the mortgage."

A shining example of the persistence of this feeling of the Negro for his church and for his preacher exists to-day in New York. The Abyssinian Baptist Church is one of the most modern, beautiful, and expensive edifices in the city; it is situated in the heart of Harlem, on One Hundred and Thirty-Eighth Street, near Seventh Avenue; although the vast majority of its congregation is made up of Negroes who are in ordinary or even fairly poor circumstances, many of them hard-working people, the church has a real splendour. The minister and his family live in a beautiful and spacious apartment adjoining the church; his home has hardwood floors, panelled walls, and every modern convenience and beauty; his servants are supplied

7

by the domestic science class maintained by the church community house; he has been given a car and a trip to Europe by his adoring congregation. The community house boasts of a good gymnasium, facilities for teaching first-aid, practical nursing, mother-craft, etc.

In fairly recent years the Church often educated promising young members of its congregation; the Church supported, and still supports, Negro artists; many a young musician has had his or her musical training paid for by a congregation. And for years, and even to-day, many Negro artists have found their important audiences in Negro churches all over America, and have derived their living therefrom. It was, and is possible for a Negro musician or lecturer to make an extensive tour of America without appearing before a white audience at all. Harry Burleigh, Clarence Cameron White, Roland Hayes, and Marion Anderson—all now widely known Negro musicians—have done this with great success early in their careers.

In the early days, when the bulk of the Negro population was fairly ignorant, a considerable amount of money and power was controlled by the preachers and the Church. Preachers, being human beings, had their failings. Some remained faithful

8

to their great responsibilities and trusts, and some became unscrupulous. The Church gradually became a complicated national organisation, with bishops and zones and annual, almost political, conferences, where many of the preachers fought to be elected bishops, or to be assigned to charges which were reputed to be rich and generous. It is significant that many Negro bishops are wealthy men.

II. THE REV. WILLIAM ROBESON AND HIS BOY

At the end of the nineteenth century, the Reverend William D. Robeson was in charge of the Witherspoon Presbyterian Church, which is still standing to-day, in Princeton. The Reverend Robeson was born in Martin County, North Carolina, on July 27th, 1845; he was the son of Benjamin and Saba, who were slaves on the Robeson plantation; it was said among the old blacks in Martin County that "W. D." resembled in many ways his royal Bantu ancestors in Africa. In 1860, at about the age of fifteen, "W. D." escaped to the North, and managed to work his way through Lincoln University, a now well-known Negro institution near Philadelphia. He prepared himself for the ministry because he felt himself "called" to the Church. He was a man of God in the truest sense. He believed in God and in the Bible, but he was very tolerant in those beliefs. His natural dignity and intelligence, his integrity, his gentle good humour and ready sympathy, his tact and his great gift for loving and being loved and respected by all kinds and classes of people, made him a spiritual leader of his people. With rare exceptions, all his Negro congregations, and all the white patrons with whom he came in contact, loved and revered him. These exceptions were the ministers who envied him his success with his churches, and were really only political enemies in the "conferences" which controlled the assigning of specific churches to preachers.

On July 11th, 1878, the Reverend Robeson married Mary Louisa Bustill. The Bustill family is one of the most widely known and highly respected Negro families in Philadelphia; they trace their ancestry back as far as 1608, along Indian-Quaker-Negro stock, and all along the line find distinguished men and women of whom they are justly proud. From generation to generation a scant history of the family's achievements was kept and handed on. They were essentially a family of teachers, and for years taught in the public schools of Philadelphia and near-by cities. Cyrus Bustill, Louisa's great-grandfather, was born in Burlington, New Jersey, on March 17th, 1732; he traced his ancestry directly back to a powerful Indian tribe;

11

one of the well-known marks of this tribe was a
definite and peculiar mark on the ear; Cyrus bore
this mark on his ear very clearly. He was one of
the most active workers for the religious, moral,
and intellectual progress of his people; he was one
of the founders of the Free African Society
(founded April 10th, 1787), which was the first
beneficial society organised by Negroes in America;
he is mentioned by name in Benjamin Franklin's
original autobiography. Mary Hicks Bustill was a
teacher, and her two brothers, Captains Isaiah and
Aaron Hicks, owned a boat, and built the first
Delaware breakwater. David Bustill Bowser was a
portrait painter; he painted many banners and
twenty-one portraits of Abraham Lincoln, one of
which Lincoln himself posed for. Joseph Casey
Bustill, son of David Bustill, son of Cyrus Bustill,
was educated in the best schools in Philadelphia,
and taught in the schools of Wilmington and Har-
risburg; he was one of the youngest members of
the famous "Underground Railroad Chain," and
aided over a thousand fugitive slaves to freedom.
Sarah Mapps Douglas and her brother, Robert
Douglas, Jr., were great-grandchildren of Cyrus
Bustill, and cousins to Louisa. Sarah taught in the
Philadelphia schools for sixty consecutive years;

12

three generations sat at her feet; she was a Quaker, used the "thee" and "thy" in her speech, and wore the straight dresses, three-cornered shawls and bonnets which were characteristic of them. Her brother Robert was a portrait painter of note; he studied at the Academy of Fine Arts in Philadelphia, and at the National Gallery of Fine Arts of the British Museum in London; he spoke French and Spanish fluently.

It was from this interesting Negro family that Louisa Bustill and her sister Gertrude came; Louisa was born in Philadelphia on November 8th, 1853. Both girls were educated in the Philadelphia schools. Gertrude married Dr. N. F. Mossell, the first Negro graduate in medicine from the University of Pennsylvania; she worked unceasingly to help her husband in his profession, and it was largely through her efforts that he became founder and head surgeon of the Douglas Hospital, a fine Negro institution now standing at Sixteenth and Lombard Streets in Philadelphia. Louisa married the Reverend William D. Robeson when she was twenty-five. She was a tall, slender woman of distinctly Indian type, with very straight black hair, brown skin, and clear brown eyes; she was highly intellectual, with an alert mind and a very remark-

13

able memory; she was rather quiet, and deeply religious. William and Louisa had eight children, all of whom were born in Princeton; the last of these was a son, born on April 9th, 1898, when the Reverend Robeson was a vigorous man of fifty-three and his wife a partially blind invalid of forty-five. They named this boy Paul Bustill Robeson. Paul was born in the parsonage of the Witherspoon church, where his father had been pastor for more than twenty years. He was a very large friendly baby, and became the pet of the family and of the congregation. He lived a placid, healthy life until the age of six, when his mother died under very tragic circumstances.

The Robesons were living comfortably and happily in the parsonage in Princeton with their five remaining children: they were William D., Jr., known as "W.D.," who later became a physician and practised his profession in Washington, D.C.; Reeve, the next son, who went into business and settled in Detroit; Benjamin, who followed in his father's footsteps and is now a minister in New Jersey; Marion, the only girl, who followed in her mother's footsteps and is now teaching in the public schools of Philadelphia; and Paul, the youngest

14

child. On the fatal morning of January 19th, 1904, the Reverend Robeson went to Trenton on business, "W. D." and Reeve were at college, Marion and Paul were at school, and Benjamin remained at home with his mother to help her clean the living-room of the parsonage. Mrs. Robeson had been suffering for years with asthma and with eye trouble; she wore thick glasses, but these had not been much help, because cataracts were rapidly growing and almost completely destroying her sight. On this particular morning she felt well, however, and decided, with her customary housewifely thoroughness, to make a good job of cleaning the room. She decided first to take up the carpet, but the stove was in the way; she and Ben conferred about it, and decided she would lift the stove by the legs, while he pulled away the carpet from underneath. The stove had a sliding front door, which opened as she raised the front legs, and a hot coal fell out. It set fire to her dress, but neither of them saw it or knew it until the blaze had caught on well and she felt it burn her feet and legs. She tried to beat out the flames with her hands, which were terribly burned. Ben tried frantically to help her, but her full skirts were a dreadful hindrance. When he realised the task was beyond him, he rushed out of the house terrified, screaming for help. A neighbour who was passing came to his mother's aid, put out the flames, tore off her hot clothing, sent Ben for a doctor, and did what he could to ease her pain. The doctor found that her skirts had partially smothered the flames close to her body and that her feet, legs and hands were horribly burned; part of her hair was burned off, and she had even swallowed some of the flame. He used quarts and quarts of linseed oil and lime-water to try to alleviate her suffering, but she lay in dreadful agony. The neighbours and parishioners, who loved and admired her, gathered at her bedside helplessly, and there found more reason to love and admire her. She told them not to pity her: "This is the way I am to go," she said courageously, "and because God intended it I am content." When her husband arrived, shocked and heartbroken, she told him with her beautiful faith not to wish it had been otherwise, that it was God's will; she thanked him for his love and asked him to see that their children did not forget her teachings. Then, overcome with pain, she concentrated her thoughts on God, and recited the First and Twenty-Third Psalms over and over to soothe her-

16

self. The doctors gave her opiates, and she lapsed into unconsciousness and died.

Soon after his wife's death, the Reverend Robeson moved to Westfield, taking his youngest child, Paul, with him. "W. D." was away at medical school; Reeve had married and moved to Detroit; Ben was at Biddle University and Marion was at Scotia; only Paul remained at home. At Westfield the father and son lived in the home of one of the parishioners; while the father worked to build a church and a parsonage, the son went to school. They spent their free time together, and gradually came to know and love each other. The boy watched his father build a church out of nothing, organise the people, bring them together, and give them a real spiritual home. Every member of the congregation loved this good man, and he did all he could for them. Although still in the prime of life, he never remarried. His work and his boy, and his interest in his other children, filled his life.

When the church in Westfield was built and firmly established, they moved on to Somerville. Here they found a fine church and parsonage awaiting them. The father and son kept house together there for nearly ten years. Everyone in the

17

town knew and respected the fine old preacher, and everyone knew the boy. The town was a small one, and it was easy for everyone to know everybody. The father worked faithfully among his little flock, helping, advising, urging parents to send their children to school, encouraging them all. This sincere, earnest, kindly, intelligent man was beloved by his flock. If he went down the main street of the town, it took him hours to walk a few blocks; at every step of the way he was stopped by someone who wished to have a few words with him. A Negro woman who was laundress for the wealthiest white physician in town would stop and inquire after his health, and he would question her carefully about her son, who was at Lincoln University, the Negro institution near by; she would give him a glowing account of the boy's work, and ask his advice about whether he should be allowed to study for the ministry; she felt that this man was really interested in her and in her son, and would gladly take the time to give her the full benefit of his intelligence and long experience when he advised her. A few minutes later he would meet her employer, and they would stop and talk; the physician would congratulate him upon his work, thank him for having sent "Mandy's boy off to school, where he is

18

really doing well," and give him a large donation for the church. If he went into a shop it was the same thing: greeting people, chatting with people. He was interested in everyone, and, because of this, everyone loved him. No one and nothing was too insignificant nor too much trouble for the preacher.

In the evenings, when he and his boy were at home together, he would ask all about the day's happenings. "What did you do in school to-day son?" And Paul would explain all about some difficult problem in algebra, translate his next day's lesson in Cæsar, discuss some elementary economic principle; and, in the explaining, translating, and discussing, fix the ideas more clearly and firmly in his own mind. The father was interested in everything he did; he was a severe critic, but kindly; he examined the boy's report-cards each month, and was only mildly interested in the good reports; when the reports were perfect he was generous with his praise; it soon became a matter of course for Paul to bring home nearly perfect cards. When he proudly brought in a card with six A's and one B, his father commended him, and said mildly, "But what's the idea of the B?" Very much disappointed, Paul replied, "Gee, Dad, all the teachers thought that was fine. I'm at the head of the class, and the other fellows are thankful if they get two or three A's." His father listened attentively, took up the card again, and murmured: "Let's see; the B is in Latin. Now, is Latin so much more difficult than mathematics or science or the rest? You got A in those subjects. We'll have to put a little more time on Cæsar next month, and see if we can't get an A in that too." Paul caught something of his father's spirit, and spent more time on the Latin, and the next card had all A's. He was very proud of that card, and the many cards to follow, because they won his father's wholehearted approval. For the remainder of his school life, his aim was to earn his father's praise; he never cared if the general average of ninety per cent. was considered fine, and that few ever achieved such high grades; the praise of his teachers and the admiration of his fellow-students meant little to him; he knew his father would want to know why he didn't get one hundred per cent. "Nobody ever gets one hundred per cent.," said Paul. "Well, what's one hundred per cent. for, then?" asked his father. So Paul settled down to study for the one hundred per cent., and usually very nearly achieved it. "What's the good of trying to get a higher per cent. than everybody else in the class? Suppose you do, and

20

the class is stupid, what have you accomplished?
All you've done is get an idea that you're a smart
fellow, better than everybody else. Then suppose
you come up against a brilliant class? You've got
to work much harder to stay at the head. It's much
simpler to take the A or the one hundred per cent.
as your goal, and work toward that. Then your
marks themselves, compared to perfection, show
you how good you really are. You don't have to
depend upon the praise of your teachers or upon
comparison with the marks of your class-mates.
When you get a grade of ninety-two, you can see
for yourself that it's a long way from one hundred,
and you know that you're not so good." This impressed the boy as sound logic, and had a fine
ultimate effect upon him; when he got averages of
ninety-seven and ninety-eight all through high
school, when he won his Phi Beta Kappa key at
college, the honours and the praises of his teachers
and class-mates left him unimpressed, and he
couldn't possibly become conceited over his
achievements, because his father would say:
"That's fine, son; you're getting closer and closer
to that one hundred." When he became a football
hero, and thousands of spectators shouted themselves hoarse with praise for his prowess on the

gridiron, and newspapers ran headlines describing him as one of the greatest athletes of his time, Paul would say: "Gee, Dad, if I'd just made that touchdown the last few minutes of the game, I'd have played a perfect game to-day." His father, who had seen the game, and had been filled with pride and admiration for his son's magnificent playing, protested: "But, son, you made three touchdowns, and nobody else made any." And Paul would answer, with a twinkle in his eye, "I know, Dad, but I *could* have and *should* have made a fourth." Later, when he became a fine actor and singer, and the world acclaimed him as a great artist, Paul still would say and feel: "I could have got a little more out of that scene," or "I should have sung that song with a little more restraint"— this in spite of the fact that he had moved thousands to tears or to laughter. He never became conceited because he was always working toward perfection. When he accomplished a really perfect thing, he was happy for days over it. He would think: "Dad would have praised me for that." This idea of working toward perfection was a great gift from the father to the son. In his later career as an artist, Paul was never influenced by praise. He was always pleased when audiences liked him, but applause never influenced his own opinion of himself. When a theatre was resounding with applause, he would think calmly: "I wasn't so good to-night; if I hadn't taken that scene so fast, I could have got just the right feeling into it." And, thinking this he would take innumerable curtain bows modestly, humbly, and the audience would think: "How shy and modest he is, not a bit conceited," and appreciate him the more.

After the lessons were over Paul would ask his father how the work was going; inquire after the parishioners, after the growth of the church fund. He would talk over plans for the Sunday school, in which he always took an active part. When he was older, he was superintendent of the Sunday school, and often helped his father with the services. He led the singing in church with his big, unmanageable, but beautifully moving bass voice, and was often carried away by the religious emotion which swept the congregation with the music. He became an essential part of the church, and, in turn, the church, the music, and the people became an essential part of him; so that later it was entirely natural that he should be able to sing the lovely music of these lowly people in all its glorious simplicity.

Audiences felt when he sang the songs that they were really a part of him, as indeed they were.

In high school at Somerville, Paul was not only conspicuous because of his scholastic achievements, but was equally conspicuous in athletics. He was the mainstay of the football team, centre in the basketball team, catcher for the baseball team, and was even active in track-meets. There were only a few Negroes in the white school, which made him the more conspicuous. He was friendly, modest, refined, very intelligent, and very easy to know. He soon became the most popular boy at school, and fraternised with the finest type of child there. He played with the sons and daughters of the most cultured white people in the town; the parents knew and liked him; he took their daughters skating, and played ball with their sons; he often went home with his class-mates to study; the parents often invited him to stay for lunch or dinner, and he did. He also played with the Negro children in the town; saw them regularly in church or Sunday school, or when making visits with his father; they loved and admired him; he ate as many meals in Negro homes as in white homes, and appreciated and enjoyed them equally. He gradually acquired a social ease that increased as he grew older; he was as thoroughly happy and at home in the cabin of the Negro laundress as in the mansion of the white aristocrat; he was equally friendly and at ease and as welcome with the children of both homes; he was a natural democrat, and had the gift of making all people feel thoroughly comfortable with him. A Negro mother who was cook in the home of the most aristocratic white man in town would enjoy serving Paul lunch in that home when he dashed in with the son or daughter of the house, just as much as she enjoyed serving him a piece of cornbread or gingerbread that same evening when he was playing in her own poor home with her own children. He went freely and easily back and forth from white to Negro homes, from Negro to white playmates, and was "Paul" to everyone. Apparently no one thought about the mixing, and certainly no one resented it; he himself never thought about it, but, with instinctive social wisdom, he never tried to mix his friends, nor force them upon each other. White parents were glad to have Paul play and study with their children; they knew from the teachers that he was a brilliant scholar, and they also knew that he was a refined, clean-minded, wholesome child, and an excellent companion for their sons and daughters.

25

Negro parents were equally glad to have him with their children for the same reasons.

Gradually Paul Robeson became the town possession: Negroes pointed to him proudly as one of their own; white people pointed to him proudly as the friend of their children; the high school pointed to him proudly as its finest student and its athletic hero. Everybody in town knew "Paul," everybody liked him, everybody admired him. He enjoyed his popularity, but he never became conceited about it; he thought because he liked everyone and was friendly with everyone, naturally everyone liked him in return. His father kept his feet on the ground and his head in the clouds, and kept him working hard.

III. PAUL AT COLLEGE

Rutgers University was established in 1766. It is one of the oldest institutions of learning in America, and has always stood for the finest educational tradition. Its historic and picturesque campus is "on the banks of the old Raritan" River, in the town of New Brunswick, New Jersey. New Brunswick is an important manufacturing city midway between New York and Philadelphia. It is said by those who know that it is more difficult to graduate from Rutgers than from Princeton, which institution is its neighbour, and is perhaps much more fashionable and better known. Graduates from Rutgers became Rhodes scholars, Governors of New Jersey, railroad presidents, noted economists, agricultural experts, and are even now important in world affairs. The first football game ever held in America was between Rutgers and Princeton, about 1869, and Rutgers won the game.

Paul Robeson was the third Negro to enter

Rutgers. James Carr was the first, and had left an excellent impression; he won his Phi Beta Kappa key, and after his graduation studied for the New York Bar. He became a fine lawyer, and was later appointed Assistant Corporation Counsel in New York; he held this office successfully and with dignity until his death. Paul Robeson won a State scholarship to Rutgers, and entered in 1915. As soon as he settled down to the routine of college life, he began to try out for the various athletic teams. In many of the big American universities football has assumed an enormous importance; it is a signal honour to become a member of the 'varsity; "the team" is a group apart—almost a sacred group. Football games are now national events, and crowds as large as seventy, eighty, and ninety thousand people view the big matches. The matches are a source of enormous income for the college athletic associations, because, of course, the players receive no fees. The students of the universities expect their teams to uphold the athletic glory of their institutions, and they give the players all the moral support possible at games by cheering and singing and shouting encouragement from the stands. In the college "the team" acquires a sort of social distinction too; they always have a

28

special table, known as the training-table, in the campus dining-room; and of course eat special foods; they have special privileges in classes, and are often excused for practice; members of the team are eagerly sought by the various fraternities. It is the secret longing of nearly every boy who enters college to some day "make the team." If he never realises his dream, he develops a sort of hero-worship for the men who do.

When Paul Robeson tried out for the team in 1915, he met with many disappointments. He was a tall, awkward boy of seventeen. The team was made up mostly of great six foot two and six foot three inch men with an average weight of two hundred and ten pounds; all of them had had at least one year of 'varsity football experience, and all had been in training camp at Redbank for the six weeks before the opening of college, to get in trim for the season; so they were all hard and fast. All the substitutes and new candidates for the team made up what is called the "scrub" team, and every day the 'varsity practised against the "scrub." It was hard playing, because the 'varsity was practising for impending games; and each man knew if someone in the "scrub" showed promise, that man would become a candidate for his own cherished place. When Paul first reported for practice, the players were surprised; there had never been a black man in a Rutgers Eleven; in fact, there were very rare instances of a black man in any 'varsity eleven in America. When Paul showed that he really could play football they were even more surprised and disconcerted, because each man realised that he might not only lose his place in the sacred eleven, but he might lose it to a Negro. So the practice games became hard-fought. But Paul was a natural athlete, a fine football player, and his eligibility became more and more obvious. Because he was the most formidable man in the "scrub," the team began to concentrate their plays against him. The playing became bitter; play after play was made against him until he was tired out; soon the plays were made successfully against him, and he began to look less and less promising as material for the team; his nose was broken, his shoulder was dislocated; he was always badly battered when he emerged from each scrimmage. But he fought on. Foster Sanford, the coach, watched him day after day, and admired his fighting spirit and his unquestionable football ability. Sanford was an intelligent, fair-minded man, and one of the finest and most widely known football coaches of America. He determined to give the boy his chance. After many days of severe battering, Sanford took Paul out of the play and put him on the training-table, to be fed up and rested thoroughly. After a week's rest, Paul was a new man in mind and body, and he went back to practice determined to make his place in the team. But again play after play was made against him successfully, and he began to lose heart. Until one day, when he was lying on the ground with his arms outstretched, exhausted after a play, one member of the 'varsity stepped on his hands for no reason at all, and when he dragged his cleats away he took Paul's finger-nails out by the roots. Sick with pain, and startled by the meanness of the thing, Paul rose with all his discouragement turned to fury, and settled down to get his revenge. He lowered his head for the next play, and when the man came through carrying the ball he was astonished to find that Paul had brushed down the interference like so many ninepins; to his further amazement, Paul lifted him up in his arms and threw him to the ground with such force that he was severely shaken up; this play was repeated several times, each time Paul mowing down the interference with increasing fury, and throwing the man with the ball harder and harder; then the coach, in order to save his team a severe battering, yelled from the side-lines through a megaphone: "Robeson, you're on the 'varsity." The team rose to the occasion and accepted Paul, admiring and fully appreciating his grit and skill. Toward the end of his college days the team came to be built around Paul, and plays were made the success of which depended upon his football genius.

In the football season of 1917 the New York newspapers came out with headlines like these: [1]

"RUTGERS BLANKS NAVY
Dashing Robeson Humbles Black's Noted Warriors.
Vaunted Power of Widely Heralded Newport Reserves Fades Before Attack of Sanford's Team, Led by Tall Negro Youth.
Rutgers Wins 14–0."

"RUTGERS BLANKS FORDHAM
Robeson, Giant Negro, Plays Leading Rôle for Jersey Eleven."

"ROBESON TAKES A PLACE WITH ELECT OF FOOTBALL
All Around Ability of Rutgers End Puts Him with Greatest and Best of the Game."

[1] The full text of the reports will be found in the Appendix.

Paul was active in other sports at Rutgers; he was catcher in the 'varsity baseball team, centre in the basketball team, threw the discus for the track team. He was always in training. When the football season ended at Thanksgiving and the rest of the team broke training, Paul joined the basketball squad and began at once to train with them; at the end of the basketball season in the spring, he joined the baseball squad. He played all games brilliantly, and the student body found itself always cheering for "Robey" when it was cheering for Rutgers. Robeson's name became synonymous with Rutgers for the four years of his college life. Football, baseball, basketball fans knew "Robeson of Rutgers" and his brilliant playing. Newspapers all over the country spoke of him as "Robeson of Rutgers." The student body and faculty were proud of the remarkable record "Robey" made for the college.

All during his college life, Paul went home to Somerville at least once a week to see his father. They had long talks as of old, and the father listened attentively to the accounts of his son's life at the university. "You mustn't forget your studies for your games, son; you went to school for study, not to play. I'm glad that you can play, but you mustn't forget the real reason why you went to college." Paul would smile and show his father his grades. His averages were usually about ninety-five per cent. and his father was delighted. The old man loved games, and availed himself of every opportunity to see his son play. He was inordinately proud of the boy, and would yell with the crowd when he made a fine play. The team soon came to feel it was an omen of good luck if the weather-beaten old gentleman in his preacher's coat was in his usual place in the stands.

In spite of his trips with the various teams, and the long hours of practice, Paul acquitted himself amazingly well in his studies. At the end of his junior year his averages were so high that he was elected to Phi Beta Kappa, an honour which few students achieve until their senior year, and the vast majority never achieve at all. (Phi Beta Kappa is a national honorary scholastic fraternity.) He was an important member of the debating team, and often represented Rutgers in inter-collegiate debates. He used to work out his speeches with his father when he went home; the old man was a fine orator himself, and was a great help to the boy; he would lovingly tear the subject-matter of the speech to pieces, and make helpful suggestions in the

34

building of a new one; he would criticise the young orator's manner with a practicality born of long experience; so that when Paul actually delivered his speech he knew it was a good one, and spoke with freedom and confidence because of that knowledge.

At the end of his junior year at college, he had to face his first great tragedy. His beloved father died on May 17th, 1918, at the age of seventy-three. Paul was heartbroken. Suddenly he was without his great friend, his dear companion, his guiding spirit and inspiration. The blow saddened him in the midst of his youthful successes. He became quieter, more thoughtful, lonely. But the fine spirit of the father lived on for the son. He always thought of what his father would have said about the things he did. When he returned to Rutgers for his senior year he worked harder than ever. When he graduated in June 1919, he had won his Phi Beta Kappa key, and had been selected by Walter Camp as end for his annual All-American football team; he was a "four-letter-man" (had won his "R" in four different sports; in fact, he had won twelve letters during his career at college, while many men were proud to have won one); he delivered the commencement oration; and he

35

was elected to Cap and Skull. Cap and Skull was a senior fraternity made up of the four men who most truly and fully represented the finest ideals and traditions of Rutgers; these four men were supposed to typify the very spirit of the university. It was extraordinarily significant of the boy's importance that he, a Negro, was chosen as one of the four most representative men in scholarship, athletics, and personality of that historic white university.

But, when Paul delivered his commencement oration on "Inter-racial Relations," he was very sad. He was thinking of his father—how happy and proud he would have been. He moved his audience profoundly, and left a deep impression on them.

When he played his final game for Rutgers at commencement, a baseball match against Princeton, he was largely responsible for the Rutgers victory of 5–1. It was the first time in fifty years —since that first game in 1869—that Rutgers had defeated Princeton in any branch of athletics. So that victory was a grand occasion: Robeson had broken the Princeton hoodoo. Since that time Rutgers has defeated Princeton on other occasions.

The defeat of Princeton had a greater significance for Paul than for his team-mates. For them it meant the defeat of a powerful rival, for him it meant the defeat of a long-hated institution. As a small boy in Princeton he had heard his elder brother complain bitterly that Princeton University never accepted Negro students, except in the Divinity School. Negroes were told frankly when they applied for admission that they were not wanted, and were not allowed to enter. Woodrow Wilson was president of the university at that time. Generations of wealthy and aristocratic Southerners have attended Princeton, and Southerners are notoriously prejudiced against Negroes. At one time Harvard severed athletic relations with Princeton because she refused to play a match against the Harvard baseball team, of which Matthews, a Negro, was a member. Dartmouth University also severed athletic relations with Princeton for a time because of the unnecessarily brutal treatment of Bullock, the Negro member of Dartmouth's football team, by two Princeton ends. Naturally there was a bitter feeling among Negroes against Princeton, and Paul felt that his responsibility for the defeat of her baseball team was a fitting close to his athletic career.

Strangely enough, six years later, Paul returned

to Princeton to sing at Alexander Hall, the great Assembly hall on the university campus. Negroes had always been segregated at Alexander Hall, and, in fact, rarely went there. But at Paul's recital things were very different. Mr. Hibben, the president of the university, many of the faculty, and a large number of the student body attended the concert. Nearly all the Negroes in town attended the concert also; there was no segregation, and the Negroes sat side by side with white people for the first time in the history of Alexander Hall. Paul sang his Negro music beautifully, and received an ovation at the end. The president sent him a personal note of appreciation, and the students wrote a splendid review of the concert and his career in the *Daily Princetonian* the next day.

At the end of his college career Paul was admired and loved by most of the student body and many of the professors. He was "Robey" on the campus, and "Robeson" in class. Many of the people in the town of New Brunswick knew and loved him. He was the university possession, and the town possession, just as he was still the possession of the towns of Somerville, and of Westfield, and of Princeton.

38

IV. HARLEM AND THE NEGRO

Emerging from the subway kiosk at One Hundred and Thirty-Fifth Street and Lenox Avenue, one enters a foreign world; foreign in the sense that it is completely different from the rest of New York. This is a dark world, dark with a vivid, live kind of darkness. The people here in Harlem are much like the people elsewhere in the city, except for slight physical and temperamental differences. But these differences are so exciting to the senses that they suggest a foreign people: the rich colours of the skin, the large, flattish noses with widespread nostrils, the thick lips, the kink of the hair, the dazzling flash of strong white teeth, vaguely hint of the jungles of Africa and of cannibal islands. The usual clothes of the usual colours appear somewhat exotic because of the contrast to brown skins. Even the speech of the Negro is different, adding to the impression of a foreign people: there is the warm, rich, lazy voice, with its soft dialect and careless

39

consonants. Sometimes the Negro-in-the-street even speaks a special language in the hearing of white people, partly to confuse and mock them, and partly to allow himself freedom for expressing what is in his mind without danger of being understood by any but his brothers-in-colour. When curious white people inquire about this "Huh-Gingy" language the Negro informs him, with a wicked twinkle in his eye, that it is probably of African origin; in reality it is merely a sort of schoolboy code casually built up by fun-loving Negroes.

Everywhere in Harlem there are Negroes; Negroes varying in colour from jet black through browns and yellows to almost pure white; Negroes with tight, kinky, woolly hair and with smooth, straight, black, brown, or yellow hair; Negroes with eyes of every known colour, and with features varying from very broad and thick, suggesting jungle tribes, to clear-cut and finely chiselled, suggesting the Greeks. These Negroes lean out of windows shouting gossip to neighbours, or just gazing idly into the street below; they stand on street corners passing the time of day; they stand in clusters watching nimble little brown boys dancing the "Charleston" with remarkable variations, some of them clapping time, some throwing pennies in

40

token of admiration for an exceptionally difficult step; they stand in front of cigar stores and pool-parlours watching passers-by and audibly commenting on them, or leisurely chatting about the day's news.

"Did you see what I saw, big boy? Did you see that sharp lookin' brown-skin steppin'?"

"Sho' did. Some sugar."

"Say boy, did you read about that darkey gettin' sent up for defraudin' the mails? He's a slick Oscar. Niggers gettin' more like white folks every day," with an admiring chuckle. "Defraudin' the mails."

"Yeah, but he wasn't slick enough. They got him, didn't they?"

"Every time you pick up the paper it's another murder or another divorce."

"Yeah, boy, these white folks ain't so careful 'bout their two-timin'."

The Negroes talk loudly and laugh loudly. There is noise everywhere—a big, warm, friendly noise. Negroes stroll along the sidewalk leisurely, making their way here and there, or just strolling. There is no hurry or bustle or tension in the atmosphere. Even Negroes who are in a hurry seldom really hurry; perhaps that is why they are usually late in keeping appointments. (There is a saying, "C.P. time," which means Coloured People's time.) One feels a pleasant, good-natured laziness in the air; one knows that these people are leisurely, humorous, friendly; one feels instinctively that here people know each other, that Harlem is not a community of strangers, in any sense of the word.

But it is a coloured community. One knows without being told that the white person occasionally seen in the streets of Harlem does not really *belong* there, that he is merely there on some errand of business, or is passing through to some place beyond. Only Negroes *belong* in Harlem, and they actively resent the presence of white tourists; they dislike being "looked over" by the "O-Fays." The "O-Fays" are sometimes acutely embarrassed when sight-seeing in Harlem; they feel very conspicuous because of their difference in colour; if they are the kind who go about frankly gazing at everything and everybody, the Negroes will regard them with amusement and remark in loud, mincing very correct voices:

"Oh, George, that's the Brooklyn Bridge over there." And the other, pretending to gaze about exactly as the strangers are doing, will reply solemnly:

"Oh, yes; and see, all the people on it are *black*. How very odd." If the sight-seers are Southerners come to "see how these No'thern niggers live in this Harlem they talk so much about," the Negroes in the streets immediately sense this, and shout mockingly to no one in particular:

"Lordy, Rastus, some mo' white folks lookin' fo' Mammy, an' Uncle Tom, an' Ol' Black Joe." If the white visitors are sophisticated slummers, they go directly to Small's, or Connie's Inn, or some similar night club in Harlem which is maintained almost exclusively for white patronage.

But, if a white person is fortunate enough to have a Negro friend to show him what Harlem is really like, he first goes to dinner at the home of his friend, and there meets interesting and charming Negroes; they may go on to a Negro theatre afterwards to hear Ethel Waters, Bessie, Mamie, or Clara Smith sing some raw, rich, haunting "Blues" in a deep, husky voice; or they may go to a Negro dance, where they meet and dance with lovely, fascinating, dusky girls; still later they may go on to the Sugar Cane, where they see genuine Negro night life. The Sugar Cane night club is as

43

different from Connie's Inn as Limehouse is from the Chinatown district shown to tourists every night from a bus. There one sees Negroes almost exclusively; the band does not play the crisp Broadway jazz, but has a low-down, insinuating, pulsing beat which makes it almost impossible for anyone in the small room to keep still. Even those who are not dancing in the tiny overcrowded floor space are keeping time with their feet or hands or shoulders while sitting at tables or leaning against the walls. The dancers sway their bodies with complete abandon in perfect time to the music; the musicians sing as they play, the dancers sing, the waiters sing. The atmosphere is heavy with close smells and wild, slow, rhythmic movement that suggests the animal freedom of the jungle rather than the sophisticated obscenity of the usual night club.

Harlem belongs to all American Negroes; it is a place they can call home; it is a place where they *belong*. When a Negro travels abroad he is conspicuous because of the colour of his skin; he is "the fly in the milk," as he so aptly puts it, in white crowds. Even if he does not actually hear the words, he knows that somewhere in the crowd a child is saying:

"Ooh, look at the nigger," or, "But what makes

44

him so *black*?" and that people are staring at him with curious fascination because he is different, because he is dark. Even in India and Africa, where the majority of the inhabitants are dark-skinned, he is still a marked man because he is dressed differently, and is therefore immediately recognised as being not one of the natives. In foreign countries, particularly in places where large numbers of Americans congregate, the Negro may not even be sure of securing accommodation at a good hotel, or of being served at a good restaurant; Americans not only take their colour prejudice with them, but flaunt it and pay for its indulgence. They very frequently go to the proprietor of a hotel and insist upon his ejecting a harmless Negro guest. When the surprised man does not understand, the American will shout furiously:

"We don't stay under the same roof with niggers; we'll leave at once if you don't put him out. The nigger knows better, anyway—*he'll* understand." And, if there is a large number of the protesting ones, and only one or two Negroes, the confused manager, fearful for his trade, will eject the cause of the disturbance. Of course, the Negro *does* understand, and a bitter, burning hatred for his fellow-countryman smoulders in his heart. In

45

some places abroad white Americans have not succeeded in communicating their prejudice, but have instead acquired the contempt of reasonable people. Independent hotel proprietors have preferred to control their own business affairs and have resented criticism of their guests, whether white or black, as impertinence. In these cases the Negro has not been ejected, but has been treated with additional courtesy; the hotel has not suffered any loss of business, and the Negro has begun to feel that Europeans are human, are really democratic, and that perhaps it might be a relief to live in Europe some day. Negroes have learned by bitter experience to shun American colonies abroad, and frequent hotels in sections comparatively unknown to the usual white American tourist.

Negroes have also learned that they must be fairly guarded in all they say to white people; they know that what they say—even the most simple remark—may be regarded as typical of the entire Negro race. Therefore the Negro is careful what he says and does; he is rarely really free to say and do what he likes. But in Harlem he is free. He can completely lose all racial consciousness; he is one of the majority; he can say something funny if he likes and know that his listeners will not say:

"The Negro is *so* humorous"; he can express an opinion and know that what he thinks will not be accepted as the thought of the entire race. He is free to be himself. He is at home. The Parisian abroad longs for the café where he can sit unmolested and sip his *apéritif*; the Viennese longs for the café where he can drink his favourite beer or *jause* and eat rich cakes; the Londoner longs for his cup of hot tea with thin slices of bread-and-butter before an inviting grate-fire; the New Yorker longs for the feel of hurrying crowds and super-efficiency in the atmosphere—just so does the American Negro long for the protecting colour of Harlem, where he can stroll the Avenue in obscurity and peace among thousands of other Negroes.

It is almost impossible for a Negro, no matter from what part of America he comes, to stroll down Seventh Avenue late on a sunny afternoon and not see someone from his home town—or at least someone who knows someone he knows. Negroes from all states in the Union come to Harlem to live and work and study, because conditions are better, opportunities greater, and the schools and universities finer than those in their home cities. There were more than 250,000 Negroes in Harlem when the

47

last census was taken. In so large a community there is naturally greater scope for business, professional and social life. Just as white Americans flock to New York for greater opportunity or adventure, so does the Negro come to Harlem, and for the same reasons. There is the Y.M.C.A. and the Y.W.C.A., where he meets young Negroes from all parts of the world; there are inter-collegiate fraternities and sororities, and other college and social clubs; there are educational, social, political, and philanthropic organisations, all made up of, and entirely run by and for, Negroes. There are innumerable public and private dining-rooms and restaurants where a Negro is an expected and welcome guest. A Negro knows exactly where he is in Harlem: he is among friends, he is at home.

As recently as 1900 there was no Harlem; that is, no Negro Harlem. Negroes living in New York occupied tenements in the vicinity of West Fortieth, Fifty-Third, Fifty-Ninth, and Sixty-Third Streets near the river, East Seventieth Street near Third Avenue, West Ninety-Ninth Street near the park, and West One Hundred and Thirty-Fourth Street near Lenox Avenue. In those days the largest and best known Negro section was the San Juan Hill district, centring around Sixty-Third Street.

48

PAUL ROBESON, NEGRO

The Negro section in Harlem was made up of only two blocks—One Hundred and Thirty-Fourth and Fifth Streets, between Fifth and Lenox Avenues, and a very few scattered houses in other streets. When the population of the great city as a whole began its northward march, Negroes too began to move north, and found their way to the Negro nucleus already established in Harlem. This nucleus first expanded to include One Hundred and Thirty-Sixth and Seventh Streets, then it grew west to Seventh Avenue. Gradually it has grown, until now the population is solidly Negro from One Hundred and Twenty-Seventh to One Hundred and Fiftieth Streets, from Madison Avenue on the east to Morningside and St. Nicholas Avenues on the west; there are Negroes living as far south as One Hundred and Thirteenth Street near the park, and as far west as Convent Avenue. Some of the finest and highest residential ground in the city is included in the Negro section.

The abandonment of Harlem to the Negro is easy enough to understand: Negroes had only to move into an apartment house, or even into a block, to make all the white people wish to move out. White Americans cannot bear the idea of living in the same building, the same block, or even the same section, with Negroes; there is something undignified and humiliating in the idea. This feeling may be a hangover from slavery days, when not even the poorest and meanest white trash lived in or too near the Negro quarter. However, the moment a Negro family moved into a building all the white tenants promptly moved out. Negroes, with their natural sense of humour and mother-wit, have worked this for all it was worth. They seek out the beautiful and well-built apartment houses near by, and a fair Negro moves in with his family; he has no trouble renting the apartment because the landlord thinks he is white. After he is firmly entrenched and has satisfied himself that he cannot be evicted, he invites all his friends to visit him. Soon so many Negroes are going freely to and from the house that they are "all over the place." The white tenants become annoyed, and then angry, and do their utmost to have the Negro ejected. This cannot be done, and finally, disgusted, they all move out themselves. There is nothing left for the landlord to do but let all the flats to Negroes, which he does, first taking good care to raise his rents considerably. Thus Negroes travel from house to house, from block to block. In this way they have secured Seventh Avenue north of the park, one of the widest and most beautiful avenues in the city, One Hundred and Thirty-Eighth and One Hundred and Thirty-Ninth Streets between Seventh and Eighth Avenues— lovely tree-lined streets with beautiful houses designed and built by the famous architect Stanford White—and, more recently, Convent Avenue, that lovely residential avenue on the highest ground and in the quietest part of New York.

Fair Negroes are in a peculiarly advantageous position in the present American scene. They outwardly resemble white people and are commonly mistaken (?) for white; they can therefore avail themselves of many opportunities which are closed to their darker brothers. These Negroes have the chance to mix with and know white people in every walk of life. A white person has no opportunity whatever to know the Negro, unless the Negro wishes him to do so. White Americans are therefore astonishingly ignorant about Negroes; many otherwise intelligent white people are greatly prejudiced against the Negro in the North (the "new Negro"), but declare they understand and love the old Southern Negro. They do not *know* the Northern Negro; in the South they thought they knew Negroes intimately: knew where and how they

51

lived, went in and out of their cabins at will, kept them in their homes as personal servants. The new Negroes are the sons and daughters of those same beloved blacks, but the white people do not know where and how they live—they have only vaguely heard of a place called Harlem.

It is extremely difficult for a white person to gain entrance into a gentle Negro home. Negroes go freely into white homes as servants, and so learn all about them; but white people have not even that means of entry into Negro homes. They hear it said that Negroes go to college, that there are many successful Negro doctors, lawyers, dentists, business men; that there are wealthy Negroes who live well, own beautiful homes and cars, and travel abroad; but they have almost no means of contact with this class of Negro, and so continue to believe that the bulk of the Negro race is made up of the dear old mammies of the South, and the servants they know in the North. These "new Negroes" remain an almost unknown quantity, and are therefore not to be trusted.

Negroes are to some extent responsible for this ignorance. Being naturally humorous, they developed a special behaviour toward white people in slave days. There is a saying that has come down from slavery: "talking at the big gate," the big gate meaning the door of the white mansion. A Negro is said to be "talking at the big gate" when he is saying special things he intends for the ears of white people. For instance, on many occasions in the South, Negro preachers were forced to advocate and support vocational education for Negroes. These same preachers who held forth oratorically Sunday mornings in favour of agricultural and trade training for their people, received huge donations from the approving white philanthropists, and surreptitiously used that money to send their own and other promising children of the congregation to Harvard and Yale and similar institutions for medical, legal, literary, or artistic training, and occasionally even to Europe for finishing touches to their education. These preachers were "talking at the big gate" when they said respectfully, in the hearing of their white patrons, "Yes, suh, the Negro should stay in the fields." This very simple device of saying one thing to please the whites, and doing the exact opposite to please themselves, has worked so effectively that Negroes, simple people that they are, continue to use it.

The blacks when in slavery were the most loved and trusted of servants. The flower of white manhood in the South often left their wives, children, and homes in the care of some trusted Negro when he had to be away for any length of time; this confidence and trust were rarely abused. The flower of white womanhood in the South often gave their new-born infants into the complete charge of a black mammy, who frequently even suckled the children. These babies grew up and boasted of their love for their black nurses. Would the white men and women of the South have trusted their homes and their children to a race that was rapacious, degenerate, and dangerous? Certainly not. The blacks were acknowledged a loyal, faithful, and loving race.

But when the slaves were freed after the Civil War, the economic conditions were abruptly changed. The huge plantations of the South required labour on a large scale which had heretofore been slave labour. Many of the original "Southern gentlemen" had been killed or had lost their fortunes in the war, and the new owners were often former overseers or "poor whites." All owners naturally resented paying for labour which had been free only a few years before. If, instead of saying, "Yes, suh, thank you, suh," and retiring to his cabin, the now freed black labourer held out his

BASEBALL

BASKETBALL

hand for his wage, and perhaps dared to argue about that wage, he was considered impertinent and "uppity," and to have "forgotten his place." Many of the freed Negroes began to migrate to the North, and the Southern white man, resenting his untilled fields, began to hate the "Northern" Negro. When the Southern planter saw his crops wasted for want of labour, he became more and more angry, and began to intimidate the Negro with threats of dire punishment if he did not remain and work in the fields. This practice is carried out in rural districts in the South to this day; it was especially successful then because many of the Negroes, newly freed, were abysmally ignorant about their rights as citizens. When white labour recruiters went South to secure Negro labour for Northern concerns, offering higher wages, better working and living conditions, and some kind of independence to the Negroes, they were often tarred and feathered and run out of town by the furious white planters. "How dare these scalawags," said they, masquerading as Ku Kluxers defending the white South, "come down here and disorganise our niggers. The niggers are all right until someone interferes; we know and love our niggers, we *understand* them and know how to

55

treat them; they are happy here with us." So the
Negroes began slipping out of town on dark nights
one by one, making their way north to escape the
intolerable conditions. If such an escaping Negro
was caught, things usually went hard with him. Obviously it was no crime to travel from one part of
the country to another; equally obviously it was a
crime for a white planter to forcibly detain a Negro
in the South. Well then, the Negro must be accused
of some crime. It was intimated that the Negro had
assaulted a white man—or, better still, a white
woman. This rumour always incensed the entire
community, and often a lynching was precipitated.
Gradually the world has come to accept the idea
that a white girl may not walk down the streets
alone because a black man will entice her into the
woods and assault her. This malicious untruth is
universally believed in spite of criminal statistics
which prove that the Negro commits fewer sex
crimes than any other race. And in case after case
when a Negro lynching has been investigated, it
has been proved that no white girl has been
harmed, but that the unfortunate Negro had of-
fended a white man in some economic way.

This lawlessness has proved a boomerang to the
South. The tarring and feathering, or cruel beating

of "a bad nigger," soon gave way to lynching.
To-day the mob spirit is so rampant in some Southern communities that Ku Kluxers often tar and
feather and chase out of town some white man or
woman whom they consider "immoral." There are
now cases of white men being lynched. Where
black peon labour used to be the order of the day,
one now finds white peons on obscure prison farms
in the Southern states. Not so long ago the *New
York World* investigated the case of a young white
boy who had been held as a peon on a Georgia farm
for several years, for no apparent offence except
vagrancy. The Ku Klux Klan, which used to be
mildly disapproved of by the public at large, is now
universally considered a great public menace, and
to-day its activities are directed against Catholics,
Jews, and sundry other people, *as well as* against
Negroes.

It is certainly not too far-fetched to say that the
present lawlessness in America may be traced indirectly to the uncurbed mob spirit of the South. In
America to-day one has the feeling that one can
commit any crime from larceny to murder, and, if
one has an astute lawyer, one can easily evade punishment. This feeling is supported by frequent
cases of murderers and other criminals who escape

death and imprisonment for no legitimate reason. A great majority of Americans openly flout the Eighteenth Amendment—it is an open secret that Prohibition merely made alcohol more expensive and more dangerous. The Fourteenth and Fifteenth Amendments have never been enforced in many Southern states. How can a country hope to make its citizens respect law and order, when the Government itself does not enforce obedience to its Constitution?

It was not until white Americans heard and saw Roland Hayes, and began reading books by and about Negroes—all within the last few years— that they became definitely aware of another class of Negro. To-day they are beginning to be interested in the Negro as a race. Nearly every celebrated person who visits New York asks to be shown about Harlem and to be introduced to representative Negroes. In New York especially there is now some sort of mixed social life: interesting and intelligent Negro writers, artists, musicians, are to be met at the homes of famous white hostesses, and *vice versa*. The white visitors to Harlem were at first surprised to find the Negro social functions not unlike their own—perhaps a little more colourful; that Negro homes were somewhat like their own;

that the Negro host and hostess had seen the same good plays, read the same good books, and heard the same operas and concerts they had; that perhaps even their sons and daughters were attending the same universities.

This "mixing" is the best thing that could happen to help solve the Negro problem in America. When white people come to know the Negro as he really is, whether or not they decide to like him, become bosom friends with him, or marry him, the greatest single barrier will be broken down.

This Negro problem is not so much of a problem as America would have the world believe. The Negro is a problem because he is described as a citizen of the United States by the Federal Constitution, yet in some individual states he is placed in the impossible position of being a full citizen, but enjoying none of the rights of citizenship—not even the rights of life and franchise. When Europeans question white Americans about their Negro problem, they are usually told that the Negro wants social equality, and that, as he is a social ogre, this can never be granted. Such an explanation is naïve and empty in view of the facts: the American Negro has been fighting for years for the enforcement of the Fourteenth and Fifteenth

59

Amendments to the Constitution (enfranchising the Negro), for the abolition of lynching, for equal education (which he pays for by taxation, but does not receive), and for equal economic opportunities —all of which are supposed to be his inalienable rights as a citizen. Social equality can never be imposed upon a people; all over the world for hundreds of years people have loved and married "out of their class." In America a white woman chooses a white man as a mate because she loves him, admires him, or hopes to benefit by the marriage. She may marry a Negro for the same reasons without ever learning that he is a Negro. A white man may fall in love with a beautiful, accomplished, or interesting Negro girl, and marry her without ever learning that she has Negro blood.

It is possible that the newness of the American family may be to some extent a reason for its violent prejudices. Americans, as a nation, have no old and sound background of culture, refinement, and class, and so they are uncertain of their social position. In order to achieve a definitely superior social status—at least in their own minds—they must look down upon someone else; they must find someone to form a bottom and middle layer of society, so they can form the top. At present the

Negroes and yellow races form the bottom layer; the "immigrants" who have not been in the American "melting-pot" long enough to have become boiled down to the standard mould form the middle layer; and the One Hundred Per Cent. Americans and the very rich form the top. Just what one of the Elect means when he calls himself a One Hundred Per Cent. American is not quite clear. So far as we know at present the Indians were the only original inhabitants of North America (ironically enough, the Indians have fewer rights there to-day than any other people); all the white people in America came from some other country; all the black people came from Africa or the West Indies; the flow of foreigners into America has been so constant during the last few hundred years that it is absolutely impossible for any one person there to claim that he is a descendant only of people who came over in the *Mayflower.*

The American Negro has developed prejudices similar to those of his white countrymen. He looks down upon the West Indian Negro and the African; the professional Negro rather despises the non-professional; Negroes with fair skins and straight hair look down upon their dark-skinned, kinky-haired brothers; the dark-skinned ones de-

61

spise the fair ones, calling them half-breeds. Negroes as a whole are tremendously prejudiced against white people. It is only recently that decent, respectable, intelligent Negroes began openly associating with white people of the same class. This social mixing takes place only in such places as New York, Boston, and Chicago, and then only among artistic, literary, and intellectual groups. Negroes who entertain white guests in their homes are still frowned upon by the bulk of the coloured population. This feeling is very gradually beginning to change. As recently as ten years ago, a Negro who married a white woman was promptly ostracised by the majority of his race, and his wife was ignored socially. Notable examples of this feeling were Frederick Douglas, that idol of the Negro race, who fell from his pedestal when he married a white woman, and Jack Johnson, the Negro who was at one time heavyweight champion of the world and popular hero of both races, who completely lost his popularity when he married a white woman. Yet Negroes, in spite of all this bitter feeling within their own group, furiously resent and fail to understand white prejudice. They may call each other "nigger" in fun, as they often do, but they are up in arms if any white person uses the hated word.

62

Usually the fair Negroes constitute themselves into a Society—some sort of elegant social group. Washington, Charleston, and Atlanta coloured society have always been particularly proud of the fairness (in colour) of their members. A great majority of the "prominent families" are so fair-skinned that it is almost impossible to distinguish them from white people. They are called "lily-whites" by the darker Negroes. In any other country in the world they would be classed as white, because they *are* white; but in America "one drop of nigger blood makes you a nigger," so these people are classed as Negroes. The true situation in America is this: *if it is known* that a person has one drop of Negro blood, he is a Negro. As a matter of indisputable fact, there are thousands and thousands of people in America who are accepted as white who are known to have much more than a drop of Negro blood. Many do not know themselves about this "taint," but their parents or grandparents know. Those who do know about their Negro blood, but prefer to keep the fact carefully hidden, are said to be "passing" for white. In a recent census taken in America it was revealed that many thousands of people had disappeared entirely, leaving no trace by death, emigration, or other record, and that approximately an equal number of people had appeared out of nowhere, with no birth, immigration, or other record to show where they came from. These astounding appearances and disappearances had taken place within a period of ten years, as a census is taken every ten years. A bright young reporter became interested in the fact that in no other country in the world, except America, could so large a number of people simply disappear. He investigated the matter, and found, to his surprise, that many of the "missing" ones were from the black roll—that is, were Negroes—and that many of the new people appeared on the white roll—sometimes bearing the identical names as those of the missing ones, sometimes bearing new names. He wrote another newspaper article reporting the results of his investigations, and the matter ended there.

Negroes were highly amused when they read the articles. *They* knew that the Negroes who had disappeared were no mystery; they had not met with foul play, or died, or left the country; American records are kept too carefully for that. They knew that the Negroes had simply "crossed the line" into the white world, and were the identical people who appeared, apparently unaccountably, on the white census roll. They were Negroes "passing for white." Almost every Negro family has some member, or knows personally of some friend, who is "passing." In the beginning, when the custom first became prevalent, the usual procedure was for the fair one who decided to "pass" to sever all relations with his family and friends, in order that his true identity might never be discovered by the white world into which he had entered. Sometimes he exchanged letters with his family, but this was done with great discretion. Usually the "passing" one married a white girl and brought up his children as white. In almost every case the secret of the Negro blood was never revealed to the white world, but was well known to the Negro world. Negroes themselves usually gave every assistance to the one who had "gone over." If to-day a Negro meets his fairer brother in the company of a white person in a down-town street, the dark one gives no sign of recognition unless the fair one does so first. This has been an unwritten law among Negroes for years: one must never speak to a fair brother or sister on the street unless spoken to first. The fair one may be "passing," and if he is greeted familiarly by a Negro his secret may be revealed. The white person who is with the fair Negro will have no suspicion that the latter is anything but a person like himself—they both have clear white skin, straight fair or dark hair, regular features, and every other outward sign of white origin. The astounding truth of the matter is that the fair one who *knows* he has Negro blood, and is therefore called a Negro, may be just as white—or whiter— than the white person by his side, who in all probability has Negro blood but does *not* know it. Considering the close association, both secretly and openly, between Negroes and white people in America during the last two hundred years, considering the remarkably wide range in colour of the American Negro to-day (from clear white skin and perfectly straight yellow hair, all through the olives, yellows, tans, warm browns, down to deep black with very kinky, woolly hair), and considering the unusually rich dark olive skins and very curly hair of many distinguished Southern white families, it can reasonably be said that a great number of American Negroes have a large proportion of white blood and that a great number of white Americans have Negro blood. Negroes know this to

66

be true from personal knowledge of definite instances of Negroes passing for white, and from simple calculation. A great many white people know or suspect this to be true, but would never admit it.

V. GROPING: LAW, THEATRE, MUSIC

In 1919 Harlem had a complete life of its own. There were young and old Negro physicians and dentists, with much larger practices than they could comfortably look after themselves; Negroes owned beautiful houses and modern apartments; there were many fine churches; there were the Y.M.C.A. and the Y.W.C.A.; there were several chapters of inter-collegiate fraternities and sororities; there were Negro graduates from the finest white universities in America; there were Negroes in every conceivable profession, business, and trade.

About this time, immediately following his graduation from Rutgers, Paul Robeson came to New York to attend Columbia University Law School. He naturally settled in Harlem. Here he soon found himself among friends. Many children with whom he had grown up in New Jersey had come to New York to find work or to attend schools; many athletes with and against whom he had played while at Rutgers were now in New York; many people interested in athletics had read of his prowess on the gridiron and in other sports, and many had seen him in action. The Negroes especially knew all about him, and were very proud of the fine record he had made at Rutgers, both in scholarship and athletics. Paul Robeson was a hero: he fulfilled the ideal of nearly every class of Negro. Those who admired intellect pointed to his Phi Beta Kappa key; those who admired physical prowess talked about his remarkable record. His simplicity and charm were captivating; everyone was glad that he was so typically negroid in appearance, colour, and features; everyone was glad that he was taking up the dignified profession of the law. He soon became Harlem's special favourite, and is so still; everyone knew and admired and liked him; he was affectionately but respectfully known as "Paul" or "Robey." His unaffected friendliness, his natural tact, his great gift for "mixing," his real interest in everyone, soon made him "one of the boys." No matter how great his achievements then or later, his easy good-natured simplicity kept him from being regarded with awe; his many friends always felt that he was one of themselves who was doing great things, rather than that he was some far-removed celebrity. When Paul Robeson walks down Seventh Avenue he reminds one of his father walking down the main street of Somerville: it takes him hours to negotiate the ten blocks from One Hundred and Forty-Third Street to One Hundred and Thirty-Third Street; at every step of the way he is stopped by some acquaintance or friend who wants a few words with him. And always Paul has time for those few words. In 1919 Paul strolled the "Avenue," and soon became one of its landmarks; he was often to be seen on the corner of One Hundred and Thirty-Fifth or One Hundred and Thirty-Seventh Street, the centre of a group. He could talk to anyone about anything. He had spent so much time with his father and in the Church that he had sympathy and understanding for the elderly, old-fashioned Negro. As a student himself he had much in common with all other students; he could talk fascinatingly about games by the hour. He had a gorgeous bass voice, and could always be counted upon to carry the low voice part in harmonisations when "the fellows" got together at parties, or even on street corners, where they might be chatting and suddenly burst into song. He could always be counted upon to referee a game of basketball for the Parish House or

AS JIM HARRIS IN "ALL GOD'S CHILLUN GOT WINGS"

"THE EMPEROR JONES"

the Y.M.C.A.; he could even be counted upon to coach a team or play in a team; he could be depended upon to sing bass in the church choir on Sunday mornings; he would "speak" or sing a solo or two at the local concerts to help fill out the programme. He was a member of two popular fraternities, one inter-collegiate and one professional; he was a welcome addition to any social gathering because he was a good dancer, a good "mixer," was liked by everyone, and could he depended upon to make himself pleasant to other guests. When Paul Robeson had been in New York one year he had become part and parcel of Harlem, and was affectionately regarded as her favourite and most beloved son. When, a year later, he married a Harlem girl, he became still more closely bound to the community.

At Columbia Law School Paul ran true to form. Among the white students were boys from Rutgers, Somerville, Westfield, Princeton; there were also boys he had met at other universities while on his many trips with the teams. Many of the student body knew him or knew of him. He was immediately commandeered to play in the Law School basketball and other teams. He made friends easily and soon became part of the campus life—so much

71

a part of it that, when the graduating class of the university held its annual senior dinner at the Hotel Astor in 1920, he was a guest of honour at the speakers' table. R. L. Condon, the president of the class, who sat at Paul's right, said that "Robeson was invited by the whole class because he was one of Columbia's most brilliant men." Paul was as thoroughly comfortable at Columbia among his white class-mates as he was in Harlem among his Negro friends; he passed easily and naturally from one group to the other. He slipped into his niche in this world-known institution of learning and in this great Negro community with the same ease with which he had made himself an important part of the life at Rutgers, at high school, and in the towns in which he had grown up.

After he had won his degree in Law in 1923, Paul began to wonder what he would do. "Perhaps a political job to tide me over until I can build up a practice," he thought passively. But when politicians came to him with offers of a city district-attorneyship, or some other job, he found himself unable to accept it because of the many enforced allegiances it entailed. He must be loyal to the person who got him the job, he must be loyal to the party that kept him in the job; he was unable to

72

fully approve of the person or the party, and so felt that he could not accept a favour at their hands. He read law occasionally with his class-mates and friends, but did not bestir himself to find a job. Paul was very lazy. He was not the person to think out what he would do or wanted to do and then go out and try and do it. There was no trace of aggressiveness in his make-up. He idled away month after month, waiting for something that would interest him to come along. One by one the fellows in his class found posts, but not Paul. He often dropped into offices to see them, to talk over cases with them, but that was all. "I'll wait a little while," he thought, "something will turn up." And so he waited, and something really did turn up.

A very successful and socially prominent lawyer who was a trustee of Rutgers, invited Paul to come into the office of his firm to work. This was an extremely important offer, because the firm handled big cases, and anyone working in the office could gain valuable experience in such work. The offer was doubly welcome to Paul, because it was almost impossible for a young Negro lawyer to acquire any experience in big legal work. This is easily understood when one remembers that there are no Negro railroads, few large Negro banks, few

73

Negro millionaires with enormous estates to be managed—so there is no way for a Negro lawyer to get any practical working knowledge of big business unless he is taken into the office of a large white firm. This is almost never done, partly because such firms always have a long waiting list of applicants and have personal obligations to the sons of friends and business associates, and partly because of the great prejudice against Negroes. The few enormously rich Negroes and the large Negro insurance companies are loath to engage lawyers of their own race to look after their business affairs, because these lawyers have not had enough special experience to inspire confidence. And, since it is almost impossible for them to acquire such experience, the whole system forms a vicious circle. Only very recently are Negro lawyers being retained for such work, and usually they work in association with a thoroughly experienced white lawyer as consultant. Paul's opportunity was one of the rare exceptions, and he made the most of it. While he was naturally an extremely lazy person, and never actively sought out things to do, no one could work more intensively, more brilliantly, more consistently than Paul when he stumbled into something which interested him. He spent all his time reading law in the office, and showed such interest in the work that his benefactor suggested that he draw up a brief on a phase of the famous Gould Will Case, which was then being handled by the firm. His brief was so thoroughly well prepared that his friend used it when the case was brought to trial. Paul enjoyed the work. But eventually the clerks and other members of the firm objected to the constant presence of so conspicuous a Negro in the office, and Paul felt forced to withdraw. His friend regretted the loss of what promised to be so valuable an assistant, and as they talked the matter over frankly he realised how very difficult it would be for him to find another berth. He very generously suggested that Paul open an up-town branch of the office and take entire charge of it, but Paul felt he was not sufficiently experienced to undertake so great a responsibility. He returned to Harlem, uncertain as to what he should do next. "I'll wait a little," he thought again, "something will turn up."

His usual good luck held, and again something did turn up. It is extraordinary that what seems at first glance to be almost pathological laziness, usually ends by seeming to be a remarkable discretion with Paul. He himself has never understood the in-

75

stinct which keeps him inactive and uninterested in
the presence of things which are of no fundamental
importance to him, but which rouses him to tremendous activity and excited interest in the
presence of things which are important to his development. It is a sort of sixth sense which successfully steers him past nearly all the wrong
turnings straight on to his goal. He himself has
often sensed this guiding instinct, but, with characteristic laziness, never analysed it. "It's luck,"
he says, a little awed by his astonishing good for-
tune—a little reverent, too. "I'm the luckiest man
in the world. There surely must be Someone looking after me."

The "something that turned up" this time was
an invitation to play Eugene O'Neill's *All God's
Chillun Got Wings* and *The Emperor Jones* at the
Provincetown Theatre. The Provincetown Players
were really responsible for Paul's choice of the
stage as a career. They form one of the most intelligent, sincere, and non-commercial of the artistic
groups in America. The group is made up of some
of the most interesting figures in the American
Theatre: George Cram Cook and Susan Glaspell,
the founders, Eugene O'Neill, Robert Edmond
Jones, Eleanor Fitzgerald, James Light, John Reed,

76

Edna St. Vincent Millay, Theodore Dreiser, Harry Kemp, Cleon Throckmorton were some of its first members. The group was originated at a wharf in Provincetown, Massachusetts, by a small number of people who wanted to write, produce, and act their own plays. "To-day, after twelve years," says the manifesto of the Provincetown Players for 1929, "it still continues its original policy, and has successfully established and maintained a stage where playwrights of sincere, poetic, literary and dramatic purpose can see their plays in action and superintend their productions without submitting to the commercial managers' interpretation of public taste. Equally it has afforded an opportunity for actors, producers, scenic and costume designers to experiment with a stage of extremely simple resources—it being the idea of the Players that elaborate settings are unnecessary to bring out the essential qualities of a good play. The Provincetowners wrote and produced plays entirely for intellectual and artistic self-expression and experiment, and all the group fell to work to get the most good and the most fun out of each experiment. They have maintained this enthusiasm for their experiment throughout the twelve years of their existence." They naturally attracted people like

themselves to their little group. It is small wonder
that when Paul Robeson came to work with them
he fell under their spell, and through them has
remained under the spell of the theatre ever since.

When he began rehearsals, during the spring of
1924, in the famous little theatre in Macdougal
Street, his first friends were James Light, Eugene
O'Neill, Eleanor Fitzgerald, and Harold McGhee.
At Jimmy's or Fitzy's or Gig's he had long talks
with O'Neill about *Jones* and *Chillun*, about the
meaning of the plays, about the purpose of the
theatre. As he knew them better the talk drifted to
the theatre in general, to life in general. They felt
the existing commercial theatre, with its stock ways
of presenting its unimaginative material, had nothing to give—except perhaps a superficial kind of
entertainment. They felt a truly important and
artistic theatre should not only present life, but
should interpret it, should help people know and
understand each other, should introduce people to
atmospheres, human beings, and emotions they
had not known before—thus widening their intellectual, emotional, and spiritual experience and
colouring their lives; should help people find more
things of beauty in the world and in life. They were
deeply interested in the modern expressionistic

78

theatre of the Germans. "Why must a play be necessarily confined to three acts," protested Gene, "when the life you are thinking about may happen in scenes, or in many long acts?" Gene broke away from the conventional rules of playwriting in many of his experiments. When he wrote *The Emperor Jones*, in eight powerful, staccato scenes, the Provincetowners enthusiastically produced it. It was much shorter than the usual play, lasting only one hour and a half in all. "Too short," said the commercial managers. When he wrote *Strange Interlude*, in nine long acts, the commercial managers protested that the public would never sit through a play lasting nearly five hours. "Too long," they said. Both these plays have achieved world-wide artistic and financial success.

Paul began to sense vaguely how great plays were written. When a sensitive, gifted artist like Gene went into a community, or witnessed a human experience, or felt the powerful influences of nature, he reacted emotionally to them; because of his great gift he could go back to the theatre, and, with characters, conversation, scenes, and acts recreate that community, or person, or feeling of the sea so successfully that he could make the people who saw his play know and understand and sympathise

79

with that community, or person, or the sea as he did; and perhaps feel, according to their sensitivity, at least some of the emotional reactions he felt. This knowledge gave Paul an entirely new conception of the theatre. As a spectator and as an actor it meant infinitely more to him. He could now get more from a play and give more to a play.

There were many long, lazy, fascinating talks. Gene had been nearly all over the world, had seen and done many interesting things; they all knew many interesting people—among them some of the great personalities of the present. Paul would listen eagerly for hours, for days, for weeks. Meantime they worked on the plays. Jimmy was vastly different from the usual director: he never told Paul what to do nor showed him how to do it. He never told him what to say; he merely sat quietly in the auditorium and let him feel his way; he often helped him, of course. When Paul had trouble with a speech Jimmy would sit down on a soap-box beside him on the empty stage, and they would analyse the speech thought by thought, word by word. "I think Gene means so and so," Jimmy would say, and they would argue and discuss. Very often Gene himself would come in to help them. Again Jimmy would call out, "Let yourself go,

Paul. Don't hold yourself in; you look as though you're afraid to move." "I am," Paul would answer; "I'm so big I feel if I take a few steps I'll be off this tiny stage." "Then just take two steps, but make them fit you. You must have complete freedom and control over your body and your voice, if you are to control your audience," explained Jimmy. They tore the lines to pieces and Paul built them up again for himself, working out his own natural movements and gestures with Jimmy's watchful help. "I can't tell you what to do," said Jimmy, "but I can help you find what's best for you." Paul was able to bring to both *Chillun* and *Jones* not only a thorough understanding of the script itself and its intent, given him by Gene and Jimmy, but also a further racial understanding of the characters. When he came at last to the performance, he never had to *remember* anything; he went freely and boldly ahead, secure in the knowledge that he knew and understood the character he was portraying. So that, at the age of twenty-six and very inexperienced, he was immediately acclaimed by the leading dramatic critics in New York as one of America's finest actors.

How complete was his success is shown by the comments of such critics as Mr. George Jean Nathan and Mr. Lawrence Stallings. In the *American Mercury* of July, 1924, Mr. Nathan wrote:

"The singularly fine performance of the rôle of Jim Harris that the Negro Robeson gave recently in Eugene O'Neill's *All God's Chillun Got Wings* brings still further positive testimony to the theory that the black man is far better fitted naturally for the profession of acting than his white brother. . . . The Negro is a born actor, where the white man achieves acting. Robeson, with relatively little experience and with no training to speak of, is one of the most thoroughly eloquent, impressive, and convincing actors that I have looked at and listened to in almost twenty years of professional theatregoing. He gains his effects with means that not only seem natural, but that are natural. He does things beautifully, with his voice, his features, his hands, his whole somewhat ungainly body, yet I doubt that he knows how he does them. As in the leading rôle of *The Emperor Jones*, in which he is a fully worthy successor to his Negro colleague Gilpin, he here acts with all the unrestrained and terrible sincerity of which the white actor, save on rare occasions, is by virtue of his shellac of civilisation just a trifle ashamed. The effect is of a soul bombarded

82

by thunder and torn by lightning. The performance, in the one play as in the other—and no two
plays were ever more dissimilar—is hot in its blind
illumination. It is not acting as John Barrymore
knows acting any more than the singing and dancing of the black Florence Mills is singing and
dancing as Galli-Curci and Adeline Genee know
singing and dancing; it is something that is just
over the borderland of acting, and just this side of
the borderland of life and reality. Its essence is un-
graspable in print. It is of the invisible colour of
Ambrose Bierce's *Damned Thing*, and of the criti-
cally elusive quality of certain passages in Stornd-
berg's *Dream Play*, or in Hugo Wolf's opera, *Der
Corregidor*.

"Robeson is a university graduate, has a degree
or two, and is a member of Phi Beta Kappa. It is
therefore argued by some that he is the admirable
actor he is because he is an educated and intelligent
man—as if education and intelligence made good
actors. Salvini, as great an actor as ever lived,
boasted proudly of his lack of education. 'An educated actor,' he observed, 'is as much an anomaly
as an ignorant scientist.' And Coquelin: 'No intelligence, except intelligence of his part, is indispen-
sable to an actor.' The Negro Opal Cooper hasn't

Robeson's education, yet there are few better actors on our white stage. . . . I do not like the phrase 'natural-born actor' any better than the next man; but, if ever there was one, I present to the convention the name of Mr. Paul Robeson."

Mr. Stallings was equally enthusiastic. In an article written a month after the production of *Chillun* and published in the *New York World* of June 21st, 1924, he said:

"Regardless of the listless things said about the play at the Provincetown, here are a few things that have been said about Paul Robeson. It seems that Robeson was a famous athlete and a prime student at Rutgers, and that since his college years, which he left full of glory, he has been engaged in a number of activities. He played the rôle Charles Gilpin, another Negro, had created in *The Emperor Jones*. It was a question that he was not better than even the talked-of Gilpin in the rôle. In fact, a great many competent judges have said that he rose to a power and dignity overshadowing Gilpin's. . . . Now, in the present play there is no doubt of his ability. Ability in application to Robeson's work as the Negro in *All God's Chillun* is a wretched

84

word. The man brings a genius to the piece. What other player on the American stage has his great, taut body—the swinging grace and litheness of the man who, with a football under his arm, side-stepped half the broken fields of the East? And who has a better voice for tragedy than this actor, whose tone and resonance suggest nothing so much as the dusky, poetic quality of a Negro spiritual, certainly the most tragic utterances in American life? And if one doubts that a haphazard Negro actor engaged for one fleeting rôle and at an obscure, stuffy little hell-box of a theatre has the intellectual equipment of a great player, one has three answers. Firstly, one can satisfy the pedant by Robeson's Phi Beta Kappa key. Secondly, there is the intellectual force of the great athlete. It is all very well to scout the supposition that athletes have brains, a very easy thing to do now that the Greeks of the Olympiads are dead, and great actors can nowadays cover their protruding bellies with fawnskin waistcoats. The most satisfying answer is in Robeson's interpretation of the rôle. It would have been easy for him to have played his colour a little nearer to mawkishness audiences are fed upon. But there was never a moment's relaxation in sensitiveness. Always there was that hard, glit-

85

tering quality of O'Neill, the dramatist with the
wallop of a mule behind the sudden caprice of his
ideas. Robeson's reading of the O'Neill figure is as
fine a thing as has been done in the Broadway
year. . . .

"But must Robeson only appear as an actor
when O'Neill writes a Negro play? It is possible
that he could do something else for the stage. One
asks the question not caring a whoop in particular
for the problem of race. Solely interested in Robeson's great qualities and in the stage, one wonders
if he will play Othello some day with a Desdemona
as capable, shy, as Miss Cowl might play it, and
thirded by an Iago as sinister as the memory of
John Barrymore's Richard the Third can suggest?
Shakespeare, any pundit will tell you, thought of
Othello as a Negroid type. After seeing Robeson's
performance in *All God's Chillun*, one can imagine
that Shakespeare must have thought of Robeson."

Even more gratifying and encouraging than the
generous praise of the critics was a note written by
his friend on the fly-leaf of the book containing his
plays:

"In gratitude to Paul Robeson, in whose interpretation of Brutus Jones I have found the most complete satisfaction an author can get—that of seeing his creation born into flesh and blood; and in whose creation of Jim Harris in my *All God's Chillun Got Wings* I found not only complete fidelity to my intent under trying circumstances, but, beyond that, true understanding and racial integrity. Again with gratitude and friendship.—EUGENE O'NEILL, 1925."

This book is now one of Paul's most treasured possessions.

With his success in the plays Paul's interest in the theatre grew. He loved the life and the spirit of the group in Macdougal Street. Their freedom of mind, their friendliness, their informality, their complete lack of any kind of routine or system or efficiency in its irritating sense, charmed him at first, and then appealed to him deeply. Their leisurely, lazy life suited his own temperament perfectly. Their lives seemed to be one long round of lunches or dinners or suppers in the little food shops in "The Village," where prices were very moderate and the food and wine or beer excellent, and where one could sit indefinitely and talk, and greet friends and talk some more—sometimes even the proprietor joining in the discussion; and innumerable parties in the theatre sitting-room, or in the studio or flat of one of "the crowd." Yet how they worked when anything was to be done. Gene would disappear completely while he was writing a play. When a play was to be put on, all hands galvanised into action; every member of the group would report personally, and perhaps bring friends to help do the work; everyone lent a hand wherever he or she could; circulars were planned, printed, addressed, and mailed; mailing lists checked over; scenery constructed and painted; lighting systems worked out; costumes planned and executed; the box office and telephones attended regularly. No one was too important to run errands, and no one was too unimportant to give valuable suggestions. Sewing machines hummed, telephones rang, gay voices buzzed all day and evening for weeks in the theatre before an opening. Jimmy worked relentlessly whipping the play into shape; everyone reported promptly for rehearsals and worked seriously and eagerly. Then, after the successful opening, everyone would join in the inevitable party of celebration; the round of sociable meals, parties, and long, lazy talks about everything under the sun would begin again.

88

The life appealed to Paul tremendously. He could be happy doing this kind of work; it was serious, worth while, important work, and yet it was fun. Apparently he could act—everyone said he could—Jimmy, Gene, critics, audiences, and last, but most important, his precious instinct which always guided him, told him that he was on the right road. He had to use every bit of his brain and his talents for the work, but the result was well worth the effort; it was thrilling and satisfying. Then, after the work was done, there was the leisurely, interesting life again and the fascinating people to talk and listen to. He formed many interesting and enduring friendships indirectly through his work, among them Carl Van Vechten, Heywood Broun, Glenway Westcott, Emma Goldman, Niles Spencer, Arthur Lee, Antonio Salemme, and others. Antonio Salemme wanted to do a figure of him. "But I couldn't pose for a sculptor," protested Paul, "I don't know how." Tony answered, amused, "Good Lord, you don't have to *pose*—all you have to do is just stand there, and the figure will just happen. You are a great person," he said simply; "you've got a beautiful body, a beautiful mind, and a beautiful soul." Humbly, "I'd love to see how much of you I can work into a bronze figure. Please let me

89

try." They worked all summer on the life-sized figure. The hot days of June and July found Paul posing, nude, with his arms raised, and Tony, in cool khaki, hard at work in the studio. The studio overlooked the fresh green of Washington Square, and was large and bare and restful. When they grew tired Paul slipped into an old bath-robe of Tony's which caught him at the knees, and Tony turned his attention to the coffee. Tony's delicious coffee always seemed a miracle; he brewed it in an old saucepan, adding new grounds to the old, which had been carefully saved, covered the whole with cold water, and cooked it over an incredibly low flame for a long time, then he boiled it hard for exactly one minute, and it was done. There was always rich cream, though neither of them had any money. (Few of the crowd ever had much money, yet they always managed to make the theatre go, to do things they liked, to travel, and to have a hilariously good time.) After they had enjoyed their coffee they returned to work again, Tony whiling away the long hours talking about art. "The human form is beautiful; we talk about the mind, the soul, the spirit; we don't *know* about them. If they really exist they exist in the body, they must have come down through the ages and

90

will go on to eternity through the body; life itself is controlled by the body, is perpetuated by the body; the body is supremely important in the scheme of things. The nude body is beautiful; its lines may suggest full, glowing life, or dormant, empty life; the muscles may suggest fine, free, powerful movement, flowing, graceful movement, or calm stillness and peace. The body has harmony, rhythm, and infinite meaning; it should be worshipped." And Tony would fall silent, occupied with his work and his thoughts. Paul wondered why anyone had ever been ashamed of his body. Paul would often sing as they worked, sometimes trying out this song or that, experimenting with various vocal effects, learning songs; sometimes just singing because the mood demanded song. Tony always worked better when Paul sang.

Perhaps in the middle of an afternoon neither Paul nor Tony felt like working. "Let's go up and see an exhibit," Tony would suggest, and they would climb on a bus together like two children— Tony with no hat at all, Paul with his tucked under the seat. Paul always remembered those afternoons in the cool quiet galleries. Pictures began to mean something to him. "Start looking at the picture here," said Tony, indicating a focal point, "then see how your eye travels along without a break; or start here and your eye travels this way. Look at those greens: the green dress, the green cloth, the green bowl, the green leaves—all very different shades, but harmonising perfectly." Paul learned that a good picture had form and rhythm. "Now look at this Rembrandt and this Jan Steen; you actually *know* these people." And Paul, eager and quick to learn, would reply: "Why, I *do* know this old Dutch woman; she is motherly and kind, she believes in her country, she is comfortably rich, everybody likes her—I like her myself. That fellow is boisterous and jolly and very hospitable and generous; he is good to his family and friends, and is warm-hearted. I know him too; I can hear him sing a toast in a lusty voice as he treats the crowd to a drink." Tony nodded approvingly. "That's a purpose of art: it should help us see and know and understand each other; it should broaden our experience; it should connect up the ages, the present and the future. Do you realise that these two people were painted more than three hundred years ago, thousands of miles away from here, and yet we know them well?" After several hours of wandering about they would return to the studio and to work. Sometimes Paul would take Tony off to a

92

baseball game at the Polo Grounds, and then indeed they were like two children. They sat in the stands eating ice-cream cones and hot-dogs, Paul explaining all the fine points of the game, and remembering the tricks he had worked out when he was catcher for the 'varsity at Rutgers. The muscular "winding-up" of the pitcher's arm, the fine body-muscle control shown in the expert fielding, the figure of the batter as he stood poised to receive the ball, struck it, then raced for the base—all fascinated Tony. They would return to the studio rested and refreshed.

All day, as they worked, people would drop in at the studio and the talk would continue. Tony worked better if people he liked were about. Arthur Lee came in often from his studio near by to talk about the figure he was executing, and which later was bought by the Metropolitan Art Museum in New York. He and Tony argued about sculpture. Arthur praised or criticised his progress on the figure. Paul learned more by listening to their discussions than he could have from months of reading and study. Glenway Westcott came in from his rooms next door very happy over the favourable criticism of his first book, *The Apple of the Eye,* just published, and full of plans for his next book. "I'd love to go to live in France a year or two, to get away from the American scene, and write my book about Wisconsin." But he had no money; no one had any money. But the money came, he went to France, and he wrote the book. Vilhjalmur Stefanson, the intrepid Arctic explorer, came in frequently. He talked about the new part of the world he had helped to prove existed. "It's quite livable up there; the people are sturdy and kind and friendly; they never bathe and yet they have beautiful skins; they oil themselves as a protection against the bitter cold; their diet is of concentrated foods and includes a lot of fat to keep up their body temperature." Stef's talk drifted on, opening up a new world for Paul, a new conception of territory, people, and ways of living. Niles Spencer dropped in and talked about his painting. "I think I'll go up to Provincetown and work in my old hut there. Wish I could go to Bermuda or Spain or somewhere; feel I need a change of scene." He went off to Provincetown, and later to Bermuda, and still later to Spain.

Often many of them gathered in the studio in the evenings. The talk sometimes drifted round to the Negro and his problem. Paul was a revelation to these people. Here was a Negro who had achieved

94

intellectual and physical honours in one of their
finest universities, yet he had retained all his racial
qualities. It was easy to talk to him because he had
none of the race-sensitiveness which usually com-
plicates such discussions; he was not on the offensive nor defensive; he talked intelligently, honestly, and unreservedly about his people, was not
in the least sensitive, discussed their virtues and
faults and the probable reasons for them; and
talked about his hopes and disappointments as a
Negro. He showed his friends as much of Harlem
as he himself knew; he introduced them to his
Negro friends, good, bad, and indifferent, for
Paul's friends were drawn from all classes. He
brought records of Bessie Smith and Ethel Waters,
his favourite Negro singers, and played them on
Tony's Victrola for the crowd. One evening he took
them all up to the Lafayette Theatre in Harlem to
hear the singers in person. He discussed with profound dignity and real concern the problems and
progress of his race, and was frankly proud of his
fine Negro blood and African descent. He talked
eagerly of his own hopes and ambitions: "If I can,
with my imagination, body, and voice, build up the
great tragic figure of Jones which Gene has written,
so that that figure becomes the basis of tragic im-

portance for the audience—make him a *human* figure—then tear him down in the subsequent scenes for the audience as Gene has torn him down in the script; if the audience, moved by his degeneration, his struggles, his fate, by his emotions—a Negro's emotions—admire and then pity this Negro—they must know that he is human, that they are human, that we are all human beings together. If I can make them realise fully the pitiful struggle of Jim Harris and reduce them to tears for him at the end—weeping because a Negro has suffered—I will have done something to make them realise, even if only subconsciously and for a few moments, that Negroes are the same kind of people they themselves are, suffer as they suffer, weep as they weep; that all this arbitrary separation because of colour is unimportant—that we are all human beings. If some day I can play *Othello* as Shakespeare wrote it, bring to the stage the nobility, sympathy, and understanding Shakespeare put into the play, I will make the audience know that he was not just a dark, foreign brute of three hundred years ago in far-off Venice who murdered a beautiful, innocent white girl, but that he was a fine, noble, tragic human figure ruined by the very human weakness of jealousy. And with my music,

96

if I can recreate for an audience the great sadness of the Negro slave in 'Sometimes I Feel Like a Motherless Child,' or if I make them know the strong, gallant convict of the chain-gang, make them feel his thirst, understand his naïve boasting about his strength, feel the brave gaiety and sadness in 'Water Boy': if I can explain to them the simple, divine faith of the Negro in 'Weepin' Mary' —then I shall increase their knowledge and understanding of my people. They will sense that we are moved by the same emotions, have the same beliefs, the same longings—that we are all human together. That will be something to work for, something worth doing." Paul talked on eagerly, finding himself, crystallising his thoughts by giving them voice. "I never knew anything definite about the sea except that it was cool in summer, great for swimming, and to be feared because one might drown in it—until I saw Gene's sea plays; then I began to really know something about the sea; to sense its power, its fascination, its romance, its beauty, its tragedy, its peace. Now, if I can teach my audiences who know almost nothing about the Negro, to know him through my songs and through my rôles, as I have learned to know the sea without ever having been actually near it—then I will feel

97

that I am an artist, and that I am using my art for myself, for my race, for the world." Then Paul would go over to the half-finished plaster figure of himself in the corner of the studio, stand up beside it, and sing, sometimes for more than an hour. The little group scattered about the smoke-filled room on the floor, divans, chairs, or against the walls would relax under the spell of his great, soft voice, be thrilled by the almost barbaric rhythm, or moved unbearably by the stark simplicity of feeling in the songs. "I enjoy singing to you," he would say simply, "you seem to get more than the voice, the music, the words; you know what I'm thinking, what I mean, what I feel when I sing." Paul felt the Negro had something definite to contribute to art, particularly to music and the theatre: his quality of voice, his temperament, his vivid imagination, his virility of spirit—all peculiarly racial. He hoped for the development of a definite Negro culture. "It would be splendid if Negroes would write books and plays and music about themselves."

This group soon grew to love Paul, and he them. They adored his easy good-nature, his simplicity, his modesty; they admired his intelligence and his great talents; they respected his dignity, and loved his singing soul. To-day he numbers many of them among his dearest friends. Before he knew it he had slipped into his precious place among the Provincetowners, just as he had at Columbia, in Harlem, at Rutgers, in his New Jersey towns; he was one of the group, and was "Paul" to them all.

His step from the theatre into the concert hall was a natural one; his friends, and even the critics who had reviewed his performances, had long admired and spoken enthusiastically about his beautiful voice. So when, after long months of enforced idleness because there were no suitable plays in which he could act, someone suggested that he give a concert of his Negro music in conjunction with Lawrence Brown, this suggestion received immediate and important support from all his wide circle of friends. "We'll have the concert at our larger theatre, the Greenwich Village Theatre," said the Provincetowners. It was just the sort of thing they enjoyed doing. Paul was one of themselves, the concert was an artistic experiment, it was something about which they could be honestly enthusiastic. Fitzy arranged to let him have the theatre for the bare cost of operation; Jimmy and Gig arranged the stage and the lights to show him off to best advantage; Stella Hanau and Katherine Gay arranged for all the advertising, printing, circulars, mailing lists, posters. The entire concert was arranged on Provincetown credit. Carl Van Vechten, one of Paul's dearest friends, wrote many personal letters to the most influential of his friends advising them to hear this new and interesting singer. Heywood Broun, another very dear friend, printed the following article in his column, "It Seems To Me," in the *New York World* of April 18th, 1925, the morning before the concert:

"I have heard Paul Robeson sing many times, and I want to recommend this concert to all those who like to hear spirituals. It seems to me that Robeson does a little better with such a song than anyone else I know; he is closer, I think, to the fundamental spirit of the music. Into the voice of Robeson there comes every atom of the passionate feeling which inspired the unknown composers of these melodies. If Lawrence Brown's arrangement of 'Joshua Fit de Battle ob Jericho' does not turn out to be one of the most exciting experiences in your life, write and tell me about it."

The distinguished Negro writer, Walter White, another of Paul's very dear friends, worked untiringly for the success of the concert. He talked to his many friends, both white and coloured, and interested them all in Paul and in his work; he used the

Associated Negro Press, to which he had free access, to broadcast the event from one end of the country to the other. Walter was one of those rare beings, a loyal and consistent friend; he often left his own very important work to take Paul downtown to meet people he thought would be interested in him. If he and Gladys, his beautiful wife, entertained guests of any special interest or importance, they always took care to include Paul. It was through Walter that Paul met Carl, Heywood, Konrad Bercovici, the Van Dorens, the Spingarns, and many other interesting and charming people.

Paul's friends in Harlem talked about the importance of a programme of all-Negro music. His Negro friends up-town and his white friends downtown joined hands and worked for the success of the concert. Together they created a great general interest in the event, and on that Sunday evening, April 19th, 1925, when the loyal and eager Provincetowners, dressed in evening clothes to do their friend honour, gathered in a body at the Greenwich Village Theatre, they were surprised and delighted to find a huge crowd filling the lobby and the sidewalk in front of the theatre, and to learn that all the seats and all the standing-room had been sold, and that they would have to stand in the wings to hear the concert. This they gladly did, and threw words of encouragement and friendly, reassuring jokes to Paul and Larry as they strode on to the stage, very nervous and frightened. The roar after roar of enthusiastic and anticipatory applause which greeted them from the audience so startled and disarmed them that they had finished their first group of songs before they remembered to be concerned about voice and piano; they had forgotten themselves in the excitement, and had sung their lovely music simply, unaffectedly, and beautifully. At the end of the programme the entire audience remained seated, clamouring for more; they gave many encores, and finally, tired out, could only bow and smile their appreciation to the still applauding audience. It was a memorable evening.

The next day many of the New York musical critics proclaimed Paul's voice one of great beauty and power, and his personality unique on the concert-stage. A. S., in the *World* declared that "all those who listened last night to the first concert in this country made entirely of Negro music—if one may count out the chorals from Fiske and so forth—may have been present at a turning-point, one of those thin points of time in which a star is born and not yet visible—the first appearance of

AS JIM HARRIS IN
"ALL GOD'S CHILLUN GOT WINGS"

this folk wealth to be made without deference or apology. Paul Robeson's voice is difficult to describe. It is a voice in which deep bells ring. It has all it needs—perfect pace, beautiful enunciation." The *Evening Post's* verdict was that "he gives to this characteristic music exactly the quality it has in the place of its origin." While *The Times* said, "Mr. Robeson is a singer of genuine power. His Negro spirituals have the ring of the revivalist, they hold in them a world of religious experience; it is a cry from the depths, this unusual humanism that touches the heart. Sung by one man, they voiced the sorrows and hopes of a people."

Of his second concert, on May 3rd, 1925, the *Evening Post* wrote: "Last night Paul Robeson and Lawrence Brown gave their second concert of the season, and revealed once more their mastery of the songs of their people. They provided this reporter with a thrill as exquisite as the revelation of Chaliapin singing Moussorgsky. For Mr. Robeson combines with a glorious rich and mellow voice a dramatic restraint and power that seems to hold untold thunder behind each song. His spirituals, sung with classic simplicity, have a particular flavour of encompassing some universal tragedy of spirit within the bounds of the naïve form of folk

103

song. And while Mr. Robeson offered the dramatic foundation of the recital, Mr. Brown's sympathetic singing and piano arrangements completed a concert that brought cheers from the Sunday night gathering."

An enterprising concert manager promptly signed Paul and Larry for an extensive concert tour for the following year.

VI. LONDON

In the summer of 1925, Paul went to London to play *The Emperor Jones*. Jimmy Light and Harold McGhee went with him, Jimmy to direct, and Gig to stage-manage the play. They took their wives along, and the expedition became an exciting lark. They all settled down in Chelsea, where the atmosphere was somewhat like that of their beloved Village. Life in London became very much like that at home: they worked long and earnestly at rehearsals; then after the opening there was the inevitable party of celebration, and the settling down to the leisurely round of friendly meals and parties. This time Mr. Harwood, the producer of the play, gave the party at his charming flat in Adelphi Terrace. Paul, Jimmy, and Gig met old friends and made new ones. Fitzy came over to see them on her way home from the Continent, full of enthusiasm about the German theatre, and eagerly talking about plans for the new Provincetown season. Emma Goldman was in town, and invited them to marvellously cooked, homely dinners. They listened to her talk of her disheartening experiences in Russia, which she later published in book form; they in turn told her all the home news, which she drank in and stored away to fortify herself against future loneliness. It seemed a great tragedy, this big-hearted, motherly, family woman isolated in London, away from all her friends, her work, her relatives, with only the few crumbs of news brought by occasional visitors from America to cheer her with direct contact with home. Her visitors sensed this, and tried to recreate the atmosphere of home for her. They would all soon be talking gaily about the theatre, about the Village, about this and that one. "Do you remember ——?" "Stella's got a baby, the sweetest thing ——" "Just think, all the commercial managers are fighting to get Gene's plays now —isn't it thrilling?" And so on and on—Emma happy, almost at home again. Estelle Healy had a charming house in Frognal, where she gave delightful parties. Ralph Stock had just returned from a long cruise in the remote corners of the world, and had anchored his yacht in the Thames just below Battersea Bridge. There were fascinating parties on board on moonlight nights, Ralph reluctantly talking about his travels, Paul singing softly in the tiny cabin, and the water lapping gently against the side of the boat.

A young newspaper man was among the guests at one of these yacht parties, and wrote the following description of Paul's singing:

"A CONCERT ON THE THAMES

" *'Emperor Jones' Sings Spirituals in an Ex-Submarine Chaser*

'Emperor Jones' Appears

"Then another call from the deck, and my eye was caught by the sight of two tremendous boots coming down the stairway. Size twelve, I imagine. Indeed, I believe the owner has said that his is the out-size. For the arrival this time was Mr. Paul Robeson, the magnificent six-foot-three-inch Negro whose acting as the Emperor Jones is drawing all discriminating theatregoers to the Ambassadors Theatre.

"The takings on the second night were three pounds short of the record at the Ambassadors. Mr. Robeson came accompanied by Mrs. Robeson and Mr. James Light, the producer.

"*Mr. Robeson Sings*

"About one in the morning something hushed the gay talk to silence. Mr. Paul Robeson began to sing Negro Spirituals. On the stage his speaking voice is rich and vibrant, like an organ. When he sings, as he sang last night, softly, crooningly, he can make his hearers mute with simple admiration.

"Complete Expressiveness

"It will be long before any of us will forget the spectacle of this magnificently built man, seated on a stool, his white collar and his white cuffs standing out against his dark suit and his dark face; his rolling eyes directed to the cabin roof; the soft beauty of his voice.

"These Negro Spirituals seem so complete in their pure expressiveness. No repetition, no extra verses that outlast the mood in which the song should be sung.

"It was an experience to store away among many experiences." [1]

Friends were constantly passing through London on their way to and from the Continent. Paul met people like those he knew at home; Carl had given him a letter to his friend Hugh Walpole;

[1] The *Evening News*, September 15th, 1925.

Paul lunched with him, and found him one of the most charming men he had ever met; he dined with Nicholas Hannen, and was deeply interested in his talk about the theatre, about acting, about directing, about producing; he enjoyed lunching with H. M. Harwood, his wife Tennyson Jesse, and their friend Harold Deardon; Miss Jesse was writing a book about Toussaint L'Ouverture, and Paul promised to help her gather material for it.

Paul enjoyed his Negro friends as well: he ate delicious Southern fried chicken when Johnny Payne was kind enough to invite him to dinner, or marvellous Boston baked beans as a special favour at the Turner Laytons', and steaming hot biscuits or feathery muffins soaked with butter, and honest-to-goodness strong American coffee with cream when he breakfasted with the Johnstones on Sunday mornings. There were gay motor trips in the Johnstones' beautiful car to the near-by sea-places, where Paul heard his host and friend, the famous team "Layton and Johnstone," sing to crowded and enthusiastic houses. The "Buddy" proctors helped to make him feel at home, gave him sound advice and helpful information about climate and living conditions in London. He had his Negro friends and his white friends in London, just as he had had all his life, and he loved and enjoyed and appreciated them equally. He worked hard and enjoyed himself enormously after his work was done.

He loved England. The calm, homely beauty and comfort of London, the more leisurely and deliberate pace of life as compared to the general rush and hustle of New York, the whole-hearted friendliness and unreserved appreciation of audiences and of the public at large appealed to him, and inspired him to his best work. He felt even more at home in London than he had in America. He learned to love the great stretches of parks and the quiet squares in the heart of the city; he strolled along the Embankment by the hour gazing at the river; he became an enthusiast about cricket, and many warm, sunny days found him sitting lazily in the stands at Lord's or at the Oval watching and enjoying the test matches.

There were few inconveniences for him as a Negro in London. He did not have to live in a segregated district; he leased a charming flat in Chelsea near his friends; he dined at the Ivy, a delightful restaurant with marvellous food, directly across from the theatre where he was playing; he ate at many other restaurants in town with his white or coloured friends without fear of the discrimination

110

which all Negroes encounter in America. He was a welcome guest in hotels at the seaside places where he spent many week-ends. This was important for his general well-being. In New York, when he was playing at the Provincetown Theatre in Macdougal Street, near Fourth Street, unless he dined with friends or in the Village itself, he could not get a meal in any good restaurant or hotel—except the Pennsylvania—from Tenth Street to One Hundred and Thirtieth Street; at none of the innumerable first-class eating-places could he be served as a Negro guest. This was a great practical inconvenience. In travelling he could not secure good seats in a Pullman train. The ticket-seller would glance up, and seeing he was a Negro, would declare he had only end seats (over the wheels) left; his wife would go up to the same ticket-seller a moment or two later and secure three of the best seats in the centre of the car, simply because he could not tell at a glance that she was coloured. At hotels outside of New York it was almost impossible for him to secure accommodation: "We do not take Negroes," they would say firmly. In places where he knew no one, this was an intolerable inconvenience. So here in England, where everyone was kind and cordial and reasonable, Paul was happy.

111

"I think I'd like to live here," he said; "some day I will."

The *Emperor* had an unexpectedly short run in London. Everyone had hoped that it would run into December, and Paul was greatly disappointed when it closed early in October. The London critics and public had given him a remarkably warm personal reception, but they did not like the play. "What'll we do now?" Paul asked Essie, his wife. "Let's stay here a while. I love London." "All right," she replied. Essie was always ready to go anywhere or to stay anywhere. "Just so I'm with you, I'm home," she used to tell him. They remained in London for a month, enjoying the theatre, concerts, and their friends. Then, as the bad weather set in, they left for the Riviera in search of sunshine. They chose Villefranche-sur-Mer, a tiny French-Italian town on the Mediterranean midway between Nice and Monte Carlo, because their friend Glenway Westcott was there.

Villefranche is a lovely quiet little village nestling at the foot of the southern Alps; with its neighbour Cap Ferrat, it forms one of the most beautiful harbours in the world. To Paul and Essie, lying in their beds that first November morning and gazing through their windows across the har-

112

bour to the Cap, the first glow of dawn was like
the promise of fairyland. They watched the sun
come up from behind the hills and flood the harbour with radiance, first outlining the roofs of the
villas in a clear, striking silhouette, then lighting
them brilliantly, and passing on to glint the calm,
beautifully blue water of the cove. For many days
they woke at five to watch the gorgeous spectacle
of the sunrise. "We can sleep any time," said
Paul; "this is too beautiful to miss." They shifted
their beds about the room so they could remain
lying directly in the sun; then, as the air grew
warmer, they got out of bed to sit just within their
balcony windows, nude, for their daily sun-bath.
Colds, sinusitis, general weariness vanished before
the magic of the sun; its warm friendliness relaxed
tired muscles, eased away tension, soothed over-
wrought nerves. As soon as they caught the trick
of dressing warmly for the cold interval between
four in the afternoon and ten at night, they thoroughly enjoyed this unusual climate: summer
warmth from eight in the morning until four in
the afternoon, then, as the sun went down early,
cold, raw, penetrating winds from the mountains;
then mild, soft air again at ten in the evening. They
went often to Nice to watch the sunset from the

113

Promenade: a blazing, fiery ball going down into the blue sea, leaving a sky of unbelievable beauty. They sat like children, holding hands, or strolling hand in hand along the sea-front, drinking in the beauty and storing it away.

The modest hotel, which Glenway had unearthed with true Village instinct for scenting the most interesting and beautiful thing for the least money, was built immediately on the shore of the Mediterranean; only a broad concrete walk separated it from the sea. In front, across the harbour within clear view, were the green hills of Cap Ferrat, with its sloping villas and gardens reaching down to the sea; on either side were the hills of the town, planted thickly with grapes and olive, orange and palm trees; beyond the hills loomed the Alps—grim, cold and majestic. Paul and Essie never forgot the thrill of breakfasting in the warm sunshine among the olive trees, travelling up in the little mountain railway, and ski-ing in the snows of the Alps in the afternoon of the same day. The Villas of the town, built in all sorts of crazy designs, and painted every colour from blinding tomato to harsh, glaring blue, were brilliant in the sun; then the rich cool green of the orange groves to rest and soothe the eyes. The informal streets were like fas-

114

cinating stairways leading up the hills to the tram-
way line, or through the different levels of the
town like subterranean passages. In a little court
that was like a cellar, Paul discovered a shop which
sold raisins, figs, dates, fresh nuts, and oranges; he
was always munching; he became a regular cus-
tomer, to the great delight of the proprietor, whose
family used to watch eagerly for him; they would
gaze shyly at him, never having seen anyone who
looked like him before. At first, the children were a
little frightened, but, under the spell of his great
soft voice and his wide smile, they soon became
friends. Essie loved to watch the fishermen spread
their nets along the concrete in the sun, and to
see the women of the town sit mending them, while
they gossiped.

Paul found his friends, even in Villefranche out
of season. There were many delightful evenings.
Glenway was finishing his book about the people
in Wisconsin; he had enjoyed writing it, and often
read whole passages to Paul and Essie after supper.
The book was called *The Grandmothers*, and later
won the Harper's prize for the year. There were
evenings of music; Glenway had a small Victrola
in his room, and a remarkable collection of records;
he introduced Paul to Elena Gerhardt by means of

115

her records. Months later, when Paul was listening to her in the Town Hall in New York, he had only to close his eyes to hear her singing through the gramophone in the soft dark Mediterranean night. Glenway even had some Bessie Smith records of the "Blues." There were long, quiet evenings of talk about everything, and everybody.

Nearly every time they went to Nice or to Monte Carlo, the Robesons ran into someone they knew. One day, strolling along the Promenade at Nice, Paul was clapped on the back and heard a hearty "Hello, there, Paul Robeson." He turned to find himself looking down into the round, upturned, dark-brown, smiling face of Claude McKay, the Negro poet. There was eager talk and laughter, then Claude took them to an enchanting café tucked away in Old Nice. "You must meet my friend Max Eastman; we went to Russia together; he's here in Nice, finishing up his book. You'll like him, and he'll like you." Claude beamed. There followed many evenings with Claude and Max in the obscure and picturesque cafés in Old Nice, or at the hotel in Villefranche. Paul listened eagerly to the talk about Russia and Socialism, then he in turn gave them news of home—Claude drinking in

116

the news of Harlem, Max drinking in the news of the Village.

Paul met an old Rutgers chum in front of the Casino at Monte Carlo one day, and Essie had to wait patiently while they discussed and rehearsed an old football game. "Remember when you caught that forward pass, Robey,——" and, "Boy, remember that sixty yard end run ——" Paul illustrated his words with enthusiastic gestures. Passing Frenchmen gazed curiously at the two huge young athletes capering about and laughing on the green, and thought them mad.

Glenway took the Robesons to see Mary Garden at her villa in Beaulieu, a beautiful little town adjoining Villefranche, on the sea. They were thrilled. "What a remarkable figure," whispered Essie; "not a day over twenty-five." "What a dynamic personality," whispered Paul; "how vivid and romantic she must be in opera." They enjoyed their tea in the lovely garden, with the sea spread out in front below them and the beautiful terraces and the villa behind and above. "What an ideal place," Paul said to Mary Garden. "Yes, isn't it," she replied. "I do all my work and all my resting here. I'm a great believer in the curative powers of the sun, and, after a long hard season of opera

117

in the appalling Chicago weather, I come here to rest and relax and bake myself."

People began dropping in at the hotel to see Paul. He began accepting invitations to near-by places. He lunched with Frank Harris in his home at Cimiez, just outside Nice, and spent several hours listening to his reminiscences of his early days and of the celebrities he had known well. "Why, when I was young," said this remarkable man of more than eighty years, "I ran a magazine called the *Saturday Review*, and on my staff were three of the most interesting and promising young writers in England—George Bernard Shaw, Arnold Bennett, and H. G. Wells." Paul dined with Rex Ingram at a fashionable restaurant in Nice, and afterwards visited his studio and listened to his favourite gramophone records of Arabian music.

One day, when Paul had gone off to visit friends further up along the coast, two charming young Englishwomen called at the hotel to see him. Essie received them, and persuaded them to remain for dinner, and over night in order to see her husband. "He's worth it, really," she told them, smiling. Rebecca West and G. B. Stern looked at each other, amused. "What do you mean, he's worth it?" asked Miss West. "He's merely the grandest

118

AS THE WAIF IN "BLACK BOY"

Photo: Steichen, New York

AS THE PRIZE FIGHTER IN "BLACK BOY"

man in the world; he has the most remarkable gifts, and he's so intelligent, and with it all so modest. He's a very great artist and a very great person. And a lot of other people agree with me." Miss Stern smiled indulgently at Essie, interested. Miss West smiled incredulously, and said, "I can't believe there's such a paragon roaming the world. You must be one of those adoring wives." "I am," said Essie promptly, "only I've got something really worth adoring. You wait and see." In spite of themselves they were intrigued. They stayed over night to see this marvel. Paul came in next morning, and was surprised to find the two very attractive girls awaiting him. "Company?" he asked as he kissed his wife affectionately. "Yes, they came yesterday." She introduced them. "I persuaded them to wait to see you. I told them you'd be worth it"; and she laughed mischievously into her embarrassed husband's eyes. "Really, darling, you mustn't," he protested; "it's awful to have to live up to all the things you say. You prejudice people against me." He turned his wide smile upon the girls. "She thinks I'm grand," he explained apologetically. The girls stayed to lunch, to dinner, and over night again. Glenway joined them for dinner, and they all made a party of the

119

meal. Afterwards they went into the hotel sitting-room for coffee, liqueurs, and talk. In the midst of the talk something went wrong with the lights and the hotel was suddenly plunged into darkness. As the murmurs of surprise and confusion arose, Paul raised his voice and began to sing. He sang for half an hour; everyone listened breathlessly. When the lights went up again, they disclosed the proprietor of the hotel, his wife and daughter, standing in the doorway in attitudes of rapt attention. "Nevaire have we heard anything so beautiful," they said. "It is like the voice of angels." Rebecca turned to Essie: "It's been more than worth staying over for. You're right, and you're lucky, and I'm glad you know it. Of course, we didn't believe a word of your raving, but it's all true. He's wonderful." "G. B." nodded her approval. "It's been a great experience," she said. Essie was glad they had appreciated her Paul. "I told you so," she said proudly.

One morning Essie disturbed the quiet of Villefranche by washing her hair and sitting on her balcony to dry it in the sun. Glenway, passing beneath, looked up and saw her. "What's the matter with your hair?" he called. "Nothing," she called back. "I've just washed it." "But what makes it so *fat*?" The natives gathered in a small knot to gaze curiously: her hair was standing in an enormous semi-circle straight out from her head and face, like a huge black wool-silk halo. Glenway came upstairs to investigate. "How beautiful it is, and how live," he said, smoothing the elastic mass. "Makes me think of the jungle." "You forget that 'way back somewhere I am the jungle." "But how do you keep your hair so flat and smooth, just like ours," asked Glenway naïvely, gazing, fascinated, puzzled. "I never guessed it was like this." He continued to finger the heavy, soft, black, springy mass. "You see," said Essie, her eyes dancing with fun, "we Negroes use hot irons to 'straighten' out the kinks and wool in our hair, to make it flat and smooth like yours; you white people use hot irons and permanent waving machines to put the curl and the kink into yours, to make it like ours."

VII. VOICE-HELP

Paul returned to America for his first concert tour, in which, as always, he had Lawrence Brown as his associate. He was glad to be back in New York. In Harlem he strolled "The Avenue" and greeted the enthusiastic welcome of his friends with his wide grin; he visited his friends down-town and spent many happy, satisfying hours with them. "Did you see Emma? Estelle? Glenway? Hugh? How did you like England?" they asked. He gave them news of their friends abroad. Then he settled down to work: he sang in New York and in many other large cities, with great success. Everywhere he went he found old friends and made new ones among the Negroes and white people. In every city the Negroes were proud of their distinguished dark brother; white people were proud to remind him of old college, high school, or New Jersey friendships; he moved freely as always from Negro to white friends and admirers. "He hasn't become at all conceited," they

122

said. "Europe hasn't turned his head: he's the same old Paul"—and they loved him more than ever.

The two things which stood out clearly for years in Paul's memory of that tour were his experiences in Chicago and in Boston. When he arrived in Chicago for his concert at Orchestra Hall, he was disappointed to learn that it promised to be a failure. It appeared that the advertising had been seriously neglected, and that very few people in Chicago knew about the concert at all. Instead of greeting his usual crowded house on the evening of the concert, he faced a half-filled auditorium when he strode on to the stage. Then and there, as he bowed his acknowledgment, to the welcoming applause, he made up his mind to give these few people as fine a recital as he possibly could. He forgot his usual nervousness. "I'll repay them for coming out in this bitter cold and snow to an almost unannounced concert; they are game; they've earned something good." He took the audience into his confidence with his wide smile, and the recital became an intimate personal affair. He sang divinely. He forgot his voice, his programme, everything except that he wanted to please these people. Critics remained until the end, and helped shout

123

for encores. The next day Paul was startled when he read the reviews of the recital in the Chicago papers (of February 11th, 1926) and found that the first music critics of Chicago acclaimed his as one of the great voices of the time.

A typical tribute was that of Glenn Dillaid Gunn in the *Chicago Herald-Examiner*:

"I have just heard the finest of all Negro voices and one of the most beautiful in the world, and those fortunate ones who were present last night in Orchestra Hall, when Paul Robeson made his first Chicago appearance, will testify that I do not exaggerate. In the soft mellow resonance, in sympathetic appeal, in its organ-like ease and power, it is distinguished among the great voices of the present. By quality alone it exercises a spell that is inescapable. Long before he had finished his first group of spirituals, Robeson had moved his listeners to tears, to laughter, and to shouted demands for repetition. His programme was limited to the music of his race. Such a programme might easily become monotonous, but this singer practises a simplicity, a sincerity, and an unconscious dignity of style that immediately wins the respectful attention of his listeners. After the first phrase from his magnificent voice they are won completely. Criti-

124

cism is silent before such beauty. His associate, Lawrence Brown, is a gifted accompanist, a resourceful arranger of the music of his people, and at times a capable vocal collaborator."

Karleton Hackett, in the *Chicago Evening Post*, said that "his way of singing . . . reaches an elemental something that sets the heart-strings vibrating." Edward Moore, in the *Chicago Daily Tribune*, described his voice as "undoubtedly the mellowest, gentlest, most appealing voice of the year. . . . It never rumbled, never seemed to grow loud, it was always velvety, but it filled the whole expanse of Orchestra Hall, and always had an ingenious charm of quality that disarmed you." Hermann Devries, in the *Chicago Evening American*, said: "These two men are genuine artists—and their singing (to Brown's playing) is something more than art, while it is as well delightful and stimulating diversion. They merely sing with tremendous vitality, delicacy, and poetry; and they carry the public with them every step of the way. Robeson has a sonorous, healthy, full-toned bassocantante which responds easily to demands for expressive quality or shades of dynamics. . . . His diction is so clear and intelligible that one needs no programme notes, and he never mouths nor

125

sacrifices the timbre of the tone for mere pronunci-
ation. This is ideal diction."

The Boston experience was vastly different.
Paul, Essie, and Larry arrived in Back Bay Station
early one cold sleety morning after a wretched over-
night train ride from New York. Paul had caught
a cold in the draughty train. They were all three
worried, weary, and depressed. They ate a hot
breakfast in the station, then took a taxi to a modest
hotel. The hotel refused to receive them because
they were Negroes. This had a most depressing
effect upon them, and as they drove about aimlessly
in their taxi, wondering what they should do,
Paul's cold grew worse. The concert was scheduled
for that very evening. Essie thought quickly, realising that something must be done, and at once.
"I'll take a chance," she said to herself, and asked
the taxi driver to take them to the finest hotel in
town, the Copley Plaza. Here they were received
with every courtesy. With a thankful sigh of relief,
Essie ordered the boys to bed immediately, did
what she could for Paul's cold, and then settled
herself to wait for the long day to end. The boys
dined in bed, and, when they finally got up to dress
for the recital, she could hear Paul's tight little
cough through the bedroom wall. She was terribly

126

worried. Paul was frightened. Larry kept encouraging him, but Essie knew his cheerfulness was forced. Arriving at Symphony Hall, they were met by the enthusiastic backers of the concert, who told them there was a splendid audience awaiting them. Essie cleared the dressing-room, and Paul sat down with his head in his hands. "I feel awful," he said to Larry. "Well, boy, here's where I let you down. I haven't any voice at all. My throat's tied up in a knot, and I can't possibly sing a note. I think the only fair thing to do is to go out and tell the audience that I'm sorry but I must disappoint them; they will see for themselves that I have a dreadful cold. And I will pay the full expense of the concert." He was ready to cry. Larry and Essie looked at each other in horror and helplessness. Larry swallowed bravely, and with a tremendous effort made his voice sound calm. "I think you ought to try one or two songs, anyway," he suggested. Essie hastily agreed that that was a good idea, and if the songs went badly the audience would see and understand, and Paul could then make his little speech. Paul was so frightened that he walked on the stage in a trance. He never sang so badly in his life. His rich, lovely voice was tight and hard and unrecognisable. Larry and Essie

127

never quite knew how they got him through the whole concert. The audience was a little embarrassed, but something of Paul's tenseness and deep sincerity got through to them, and they appreciated that. Poor Larry was heart-broken. Boston was his home ground, and he had so wanted to do well there. Paul was so shocked at his performance that he declared he would never sing again. He would return to the stage and remain there. Poor boy, his despair was pathetic. The newspapers next day were amazingly kind, nearly all of them mentioning the obvious cold.

They returned to New York greatly discouraged. Essie thought a great deal about this unhappy experience. It seemed to her incredible that Paul's voice could be so gorgeous one day and so dead the next. She knew that travelling bad weather, and an unpleasant incident had been partly responsible, but she knew also that other concert singers had the same sort of difficulties to combat, and that they managed to sing fairly well in spite of such things. Why couldn't Paul? There must be some way to sing well, at least fairly well, over a cold; there must be a way to sing well even over nervousness; there must be some general fortification against these enemies of the voice. "Training," she thought; "that would help him through his bad times." She said nothing about this to Paul, but began looking for a vocal teacher. She felt his must be no ordinary teacher; he must have a teacher who would listen to him sing, and when he sang well point out to him *how* he sang, and show him how he might always accomplish this, even under unfavourable circumstances. Paul had no knowledge of singing technique. He had one of those naturally beautiful and perfectly placed voices which only went wrong when he was nervous or had a cold. He had no idea how he sang; he just opened up his throat and his heart, and, if all was well, he sang divinely. Essie wanted to find a teacher who would not touch his voice as such; it seemed to her quite perfect. The more recitals she heard, the more prejudiced she became against the so-called "trained" voice. The technique seemed to level all the voices to one uninteresting mould; it seemed to her lay mind that the more perfectly, technically, one sang, the less interesting the voice became. There was just a well placed, well handled vibrant voice which was so absorbed in being produced properly that it lost all the colour, roundness and personality which distinguish voices indi-

129

vidually. She didn't want Paul's voice to sink to this mould.

As she was thinking over this problem, a most fortunate coincidence brought Theresa Armitage to New York, and the Robesons' proverbial good luck brought them together. Theresa Armitage had taught singing in the high schools in Chicago when Essie had been a student there. She had admired the little girl's rich contralto voice, and had advised her to become a singer; she had even given her vocal lessons for a year, and during the year they had become firm friends. Miss Armitage was delighted to see "Eslanda" again (she was the only person who ever called Essie by her full name), and curious and eager to learn what she had done with her voice. Essie explained that she had done nothing with it, but had been rather successful with her chemistry. "But," she said enthusiastically, "I've married the most beautiful Voice I've ever heard, and I want you to help me with it." She told her old friend all about her husband's voice and about his recent difficulties. Miss Armitage had become an authority on voice training. She had studied all vocal methods exhaustively, and had worked out a system of her own based upon natural vocal principles for the individual. Each

130

voice was a different problem to her. She was especially interested in children's voices, and in adult voices which had been wrongly used or trained. She was a remarkable vocal diagnostician, and took great interest and pride in putting voices "right" again. She had a gift for such work which amounted to genius. She was also something of a psychologist, and had an uncanny accuracy in sensing what was wrong with a singer, mentally, physically, and vocally. She was the ideal person for Paul.

Miss Armitage thought her little friend was exaggerating, but she decided she had better hear this Voice. She did so, and agreed that it was the most beautiful voice she had ever heard in her life. She became greatly interested in its development, and is so still. Her own musical affairs kept her travelling rather constantly all over America, so she sent Paul to another teacher. Paul went to this teacher for nearly a year and learned a great deal from him; he was very remarkable in many ways, and was especially helpful for the low voice. But there came a time when Paul seemed to make no further progress. Another fortunate coincidence threw him into the arms of another musical friend, who suggested that he study with a famous German voice-teacher who divided her time between New York and Berlin. Paul went to her and learned a great deal more; she helped him enormously; but, just as they were making real progress, she left for her Berlin season. Paul was very sorry to see her go. But within a month Miss Armitage returned to New York to remain permanently. She went over Paul's voice thoroughly, congratulated him upon his splendid progress, and undertook the task of continuing his musical education herself. She has always remained his great friend and vocal adviser.

They had great times together. Paul's "lessons" were usually great fun. "Isn't it too bad my range is so short," he said one day. "Oh, it's short, is it?" asked Miss Armitage, with a twinkle in her eye. They became engrossed in their work, and at the end of an hour she said: "Now, my dear child, that low note you just sang so beautifully was low D, and the last magnificent top note was middle E. You just think your range is short. It's all of two and a quarter octaves, which is long enough for any reasonable person." "You don't mean to tell me that high note was E," Paul said incredulously. "It was so easy; if I'd known how high I was I'd have been scared to death." He grinned, and danced up and down in his delight. Miss Armitage

132

smiled; she enjoyed working with this great over-
grown boy. "I'll never take you any higher than
you can go easily, so don't be afraid," she said
reassuringly. She would often tell him: "Now,
Paul, *don't dig* for your low notes. Raise your chin
and sing them freely; *think* them high, and they
will be bright; if you keep reaching down for them
they will be dark." Or, "You *must not* climb up
and reach for that top note; think it low and bring
your chin down on it, and it will come easily."
And, sure enough, to his amazement, his low notes
became clear and resonant, and his high notes easy
and firm. Paul was elated. "It's all so *simple*," he
said. "Don't cover up your voice so, child," Miss
Armitage said; "just open your mouth and throat
and let the tone come out freely. Don't *set* your
throat—that closes it. Relax it, and you'll see how
the voice rolls out." Paul tried relaxing his throat,
and his whole body as well. "Gee," he said delightedly, after an hour's work, "you know my
throat doesn't feel tired at all; in fact, my voice
actually feels rested." He strolled up and down the
studio, amazed that this should be so. Miss Armitage laughed. "And now, my child, you will always
know that you are singing *right* when you do not
tire. When you set your throat and cover your

133

tones, you tire the muscles. But when you relax your throat you will find the more you sing the more flexible your voice will be, because correct singing oils the chords naturally and rests the voice." Paul was tremendously interested, and worked long and faithfully.

VIII. TWO PAULS

Darling, I'd love to have a baby," Essie told her astonished husband one day in their Harlem flat. They had been married six years. Paul recognised the tone in her voice. "Good Lord, she has already made up her mind," he thought, and knew from experience how useless it would be to argue. "I'll try to stop her, anyway," he thought. Aloud he said cautiously: "Do you think you ought, with your uncertain health?" "Oh, I'd love it," she answered, ignoring the important question. "Just think, a lovely boy, exactly like you." When Essie made up her mind or set her heart upon anything, she could never see beyond that one thing. On these occasions Paul used to say she had a one-track mind. She saw that Paul looked worried and disapproving. "Oh, darling, you're much too wonderful for me to miss that chance." Paul realised that nothing would change her decision; she was merely trying to win him over because his disapproval always distressed her.

135

"I don't like the idea at all. You know you're not strong enough. I'll never forgive you if you ruin what is left of your health for a baby. I'd never like the child. It's very unfair. I love you, and you're more than enough. I'm perfectly satisfied. I say, NO." Essie loved his consideration for her. But she had made up her mind. "I'll take a chance," she thought excitedly, "and I may end up with *two* Pauls."

She was very happy while she was carrying her child. Her high spirits were infectious, and Paul soon found himself almost as gay as she was. Her health improved miraculously, and she went about humming gaily to herself all day long. "If it's a girl we'll call her Paula; but I know it'll be a boy, and we'll name him Paul." But her husband put his foot down. "If it's a girl we'll call her Eslanda," he said firmly. Essie grew fat and radiant, her cheeks flushed with good health and her eyes shining with happiness. She would often smile confidently at her husband and say dreamily: "It's a great, fine, beautiful boy, exactly like you." And Paul's eyes would fill with tears, and he would humbly take her in his arms.

Their son was born on November 2nd, 1927. Essie nearly lost her life in the struggle to bring him into the world. He was an exact replica of his father; the likeness was so startling that it became a joke among their friends. He was an enormous, healthy, happy, peaceful brown baby who grew more absurdly like his father as the months flew by. Even his baby voice was deep. No one ever asked his name; everyone simply and naturally called him Paul.

IX. LONDON AGAIN

One bright day, April, 1928, six months after the birth of his son, Paul came home beaming. "Come on, pack your things; we're going to London." "You're joking," said Essie, hoping he wasn't. "Don't you believe it. I'm going to sing 'Ol' Man River' in the London production of *Show Boat*. It's all settled." Essie gaily packed their things. *Show Boat* was such a success and had such a long run in London, that the Robesons settled there. It was said by many of the critics and the public at large that Paul was partly responsible for the unusual success of the play. He endeared himself nightly to the English audiences with his song.

There was always some confusion about Paul's going to London. When it was first suggested that he go to play *The Emperor Jones*, the producers insisted upon having Charles Gilpin, the Negro actor who had created the rôle in America. "The play is too important; too much depends upon the

138

leading character. We want Gilpin. Who is this Robeson, anyway?" They were finally persuaded to accept Paul, and were afterwards very glad that they did. This time the producer did not want to engage Paul for the rôle of Joe in *Show Boat* "It's an unimportant part; the song isn't the hit-song of the play. Robeson is too big a man for such a small part." They too were finally persuaded to engage him, and were surprised and delighted when he built "Ol' Man River," which Jerome Kern had dedicated to him, into the theme song of the play. Even though the rôle was a small one, he made such an impression upon the London public that editorials were printed about him, discussing and praising him as an actor, as a singer, and as a human being. A typical article was one by James Douglas, in the *Daily Express* of July 5th, 1928, under the heading "A Negro Genius in London":

" . . . I went into the Drury Lane Theatre to hear Paul Robeson singing Negro Spirituals. For nearly two hours he transfigured the packed house of worldlings with mystical emotion. We sat there in a trance of noiseless ecstasy as he touched our heart-strings with his marvellous voice.

"He is more than a great actor and a great

139

singer. He is a great man, who creates the soul of
a people in bondage and shows you its true kinship with the fettered soul of man. We became
like little children as we surrendered to his magical
genius. . . .

"What is the secret of his mastery of all our
highest moods and all our holiest emotions? He
stands there in a plain tweed suit, holding a piece
of paper in his two immobile hands. Not a gesture.
He is a giant, an athlete, a Rugby player, and a
man of culture. . . .

"There were seconds when his face was alight
and aflame with seership. We saw the rapt mysti-
cism gathering in intensity until it reached the
height of the mood, and then it slowly faded like
a sunset, and he locked the door on it with a
tightened, tense mouth.

"Before he sings a note he looks at you with
his dream-charged eyes. Then, as you yield to his
powerful domination, he turns his head with a
smile to Lawrence Brown at the piano, and nods.
He has you, and he holds you in a dream-state till
the song creeps back into the silence out of which
it came. . . .

"His songs are the Bible as we heard it at our
mother's knee. They are the mother-songs of man-

kind, those hidden songs that all men and women hear whispering in their buried memory. It is not only the dreaming Negro soul that yearns in these cumulative refrains. It is the sad soul of humanity reaching out into the mystery of life and death. . . .

"I have heard all the great singers of our time. No voice has ever moved me so profoundly with so many passions of thought and emotion. The marvel is that there is no monotony in the spiritual spell. It is effortless enchantment moving through fluctuant states of thought and feeling. . . .

"Strange that a Negro singer out of *Show Boat* should be able to fill a vast theatre with a divine witchery of Bunyan and Wesley, and reveal to astonished worldlings the world beyond their world."

X. *FINDING HIMSELF*

The Robesons settled permanently in London; Essie found a charming house in Hampstead, directly overlooking the famous Heath, and brought her son and her mother there. Again Paul found old friends and made new ones. The familiar round of leisurely meals and long, lazy talks began again.

They were dining with Marion Griffith one evening at the ——— Club in Piccadilly. Marion was one of the old crowd Paul had been fortunate enough to find again in London. "Someone ought to write a book about Paul," said Marion casually, over coffee; "his life would read like a fairy-tale." Her open look was met by embarrassed silence from both Paul and his wife. "Why, what's the matter," she continued, "don't you think it's a good idea? I think it's grand. Really, now———" She broke off, gazing at them inquiringly. "I've been working on a book about him for months," said Essie hesitantly. "I've already finished one

142

version and discarded it, and now I'm hard at work
on a second one. Of course, it's rotten, but as I
write I begin to see more what I really want to say;
so perhaps the tenth re-writing will begin to look
promising. Of course," she added hastily, "I
wouldn't dream of publishing it unless Paul approved of it—and that's going to be my hardest
battle." Marion was deeply interested. "Please,
please tell me about it," she said eagerly. "The
whole trouble," put in Paul, annoyed at being
made, as usual, the object of the discussion, "is
that Essie thinks she knows me, and she really
doesn't know me at all." Marion giggled, and Paul,
ignoring Essie's furious look of disagreement, continued largely, "She thinks I'm a little tin angel
with no faults at all, and so, of course the book is
stupid, uninteresting, and untrue." Marion looked
at Essie with twinkling eyes. "Perhaps you're not
the one to write it, then," she said comfortingly.
"After all, I should think it would be rather a job
for a wife to write freely about her husband without being too severe or too lenient with him." But
Essie glanced witheringly at Paul, not in the least
impressed by his outburst; she addressed herself
to Marion: "You know, we've been married for
eight years, and we've never yet agreed about

anything. We fight bitterly about everything of importance. We have argued and disagreed about everything under the sun. Oh, don't worry," she said, as Marion's hurt surprise showed in her eager face; patting her hand affectionately, she continued: "We're terribly thick. I daresay we're better friends than anybody you know; and I'm sure he loves me more than ever, and I know I love him a thousand times more than when we were first married. He's a blessed, confounded, adorable nuisance." "That's just what makes me so mad," said Paul angrily; "she treats me just as though I were a baby or a small child; she refuses to realise that I'm a grown man." He was fuming like a small boy. "Well," said Essie, unperturbed, "perhaps when you grow up I'll treat you as a man." "Now what can you do with a woman like that?" asked Paul in disgust. "You see, she's the last person in the world to write about me; she doesn't even know me." "All right," said Essie, "I give in. Suppose you tell Marion some of your faults. She's as sure as you are that you have them. Come on, trot them out." "Oh, do," said Marion, deeply interested. "Let's find a quiet room all to ourselves and thresh this out." They went upstairs and made themselves cosy in an empty club-room.

144

"Now," said Marion, "let's have it." "Well"—
Paul hesitated very boyishly—"she thinks I'm
brave and honest and moral, when, as a matter of
fact, I'm none of those things." "I've always
thought you were most of those things myself,"
said Marion soothingly. "What makes you say you
aren't?" "Take courage, for instance. I think I'm
a coward. Why I can remember time after time in
my football career when I could have and should
have made fine plays in a pinch, I welched them
because I knew I'd get hurt. When I came up
against a man I knew could lick me in a game, I
just never ran through him, I always ran around
the other end. Sandy can tell you how yellow I was.
He could see all the things I could have done, but
didn't. When I came off the field and everybody
was raving about what a great football player I was,
Sandy would just look at me, and I knew he had
seen me miss that chance. Of course, he never *said*
anything. But he knew and I knew. I don't think
I ever went into a football game without being
nervous and scared to death." "That's remarkable,
Paul," said Marion; "one thinks of you as leaping
into every breach in the game. It's very hard to
think of you deliberately missing chances because
you were scared." "That's just why it's so embar-

145

rassing to have people always raving about my courage, when I really haven't any," said Paul triumphantly. "I can see that," said Marion. "Can't you, Essie?" "No I can't," she answered impatiently; "that's just the way he puts it. He has described plays like that to me. For instance, here's one I remember clearly," she went on eagerly, trying to make her point. "He was running down the field at top speed to catch a forward pass; just as he was about to raise both arms to catch the ball and score a great run for his team, he spied a huge half-back running directly at him from the sideline. Now, if he raised his arms and caught that ball, he would leave his body entirely unprotected, and the man would tackle him at full speed with the weight of a two-hundred-pound body behind the tackle. That meant a sure injury—probably a serious one. He didn't catch the ball; instead he lowered his arms and protected himself, and warded off the tackle." "Which was sheer cowardice," broke in Paul. "Which was sheer common sense," protested Essie. "Self-preservation is the first law of nature. He had already suffered a broken collar-bone, a dislocated shoulder, a broken ankle from such tackles, and I say, if he had left himself unprotected and caught that ball for dear

146

old Rutgers, he'd have been a pure jackass." Paul glared his exasperation. "I can see," said Marion thoughtfully, "why he thinks he wasn't brave. And I can also see Essie's point of view. I'm not sure which one of you is right. Of course, Paul is taking absolute perfection as his standard of comparison. Which is a fine thing for him." "But if I put that in a book—said he was a coward—it would be misleading and untrue, wouldn't it?" asked Essie. "Yes, it would," conceded Marion, "but still there ought to be some way to put in how Paul feels about it." "That's all I ask," said Paul.

Marion was ready to stop here, but Essie was not. Having finally brought the book out into the open for discussion, she wanted to talk it out completely, and either prove herself wrong or bring Paul over to her point of view. "Take his honesty," she said, with an irritating smile; "he says he's dishonest." Paul, feeling the undercurrent of her profound disagreement, and anxious to convince her of his feeling about himself, jumped in quickly: "Yes, I'm dishonest too." Marion looked incredulous. "How?" she asked. Paul searched his mind for a definite example. "There was the money Dad used to send me at college. I knew he was old and tired and that the money came hard, and that

147

he wanted me to use it for important things, but I spent it on things he wouldn't have approved of, or threw it away on trifles; and then lied to him about it. That was low dishonesty. Then there was the money my brother Ben sent me from the army —money I was to use to pay important bills and family debts. I knew the bills and the debts were not particularly urgent, so I occasionally kept a cheque and spent it for myself. It wouldn't have been so bad if he hadn't trusted me so completely, or if I had needed the money," he hastened on, still uncomfortable and unhappy over the memory of those mistakes; "but I was simply hanging around New York wasting my time when I should have been working. And then there's money now. We've agreed that Essie must take care of all the money I earn—she's more practical and knows how to get most out of it. Well"—he said this a little sheepishly, regretfully—"I often take out a good sum and spend it on something I know she wouldn't approve of, or that we can't afford, and I'm not even honest enough to tell her I took the money. So really, Marion, you can't expect me to sit by and let people believe that I'm an especially honest person, when I'm not honest at all." Marion looked thoughtful. "I must say I don't like the idea of

148

your doing such things, Paul; especially your brother's money when he was away at the war. But, still, they don't seem to me such awful or criminal mistakes. I suppose every boy at college misspends money and lies about it. Parents expect that." She seemed doubtful. Essie broke in, eager to drive her point home. "But Marion, if he wasn't essentially honest would these things worry him so? He has stewed so over his brother's money during the last few years that he has re-paid him twice over the amount he kept. And when he could least afford it, too," she added ruefully. "If he was so dishonest would the memory of those college indiscretions rankle so deeply? And his spending what he calls *our* money without my consent? Why it's his own money; he earns it; he just gives it to me to keep; he has every right to spend it if he likes. Most husbands keep it all and spend it as they wish and dare a wife to say anything. But, no, my honest lad gives it all to me, and then worries when he spends some without my approval. That's my idea of real honesty." "But it isn't my money at all," protested Paul, "it's hers. She helped me earn it, and she does as much work as I do, and has a lot of responsibility, and has to stretch the money and pay all the bills. So it really isn't mine." "You

149

see, Marion," said Essie, ignoring her husband, "he's talking about literal honesty. Perhaps he isn't honest by that standard. But I'm thinking of the very spirit of honesty, which is to me more important. He is more honest than any one I know, from that standard." "I see what you both mean," answered Marion, "and I must say I think you're both right. Now, let's have your immorality, Paul." And, in spite of her effort to look serious, her eyes glinted with amused unbelief.

Paul thought a while. "It's very difficult. You see I don't like to hurt Essie's feelings. But she's so unreasonable and absurd. She keeps raving about she'd never believe I was unfaithful to her, even if the evidence was strong against me." "Are you unfaithful to her?" asked Marion. But Paul refused to commit himself. "If I were to admit I am, or had been, what good would it do? She'd never believe it." "Then why worry her?" asked Marion practically. "Well, it puts me in such a false position with myself, to have her insist that I'm true and faithful, when I might not be. I wouldn't mind if she wasn't so *sure*," he went on in exasperation. "You've no idea how awful it is to go about having her convinced that I'm a little tin god when I'm really far from that. If she weren't

HEAD OF PAUL ROBESON BY EPSTEIN

"OL' MAN RIVER"

so sure I was so good, I wouldn't mind so much. But, as it is, it's extremely embarrassing to me, and puts me in a very false position. Because *I'm* not posing as a god." Essie was silent and lost in deep thought for a long time. Both Paul and Marion watched her uncomfortably. At last she drew a deep breath and broke the silence. "We might as well finish this argument, now that we've begun it." She gazed at Paul a moment, and then went on as though Marion were not there. "I know what you mean about your being unfaithful to me, but you don't know what I mean. So we're really talking about quite different things—as we often do." Paul was completely interested, and felt that at last the sore point would be cleared up. "You mean that some one may have fascinated you and interested you tremendously, and that you consummated that interest. Let's suppose you did. Would it shock you to learn that I might have suspected as much? Of course, I'm not admitting anything, even now. Why should I admit bad news, if it might not be true. But if I suspected you, I remembered at the same time that in the eight years of our marriage I have been desperately ill three times, with long tedious convalescences following each illness; I remembered that we have been separated

151

for long intervals by your work. Well, darling,"
she said, looking at him tenderly, "if I ever thought
there were lapses, I thought of the possible reasons
for them, and dismissed them as not lapses at all.
But what I am thoroughly convinced of is this:
that no matter what you may have done in these
eight years, there has been no change whatever in
your love for me—except perhaps that it has increased. I know that you are faithful to me in the
all important spirit of things; that I am the one
woman in your life, in your thoughts, in your love.
No matter what other women may have been to
you, and you to them, they have in no way walked
in my garden. We have kept that sacred to us. I'm
not a fool. I love you so much, and understand you
so well, and have been so close to you all these
years, that I should have known, I should have felt,
if you were in any way slipping from me. If there
have been others, they have, strangely enough,
brought us closer together." Paul's eyes were full
of tears, and full of an immense relief. They had
forgotten Marion. They had settled a point which
had rankled in their hearts for a long time. After
a while Marion brought the happy silence to an
end with a discreet cough. "It seems, again, you're
both right. In your mind, Paul, you're unfaithful;

in Essie's mind you're the most faithful of husbands." Paul, deeply stirred, said, with an effort at lightness, "What can you do with a woman like that?" And he gave his wife a long look, full of deep respect and understanding affection.

Later, when they had reached home, neither wanted to go in. They felt their new understanding was too grand to be enclosed within four walls. "Let's take a walk," said Essie. "All right," agreed Paul, "and talk some more." They stood for a moment looking at the open Heath rolling out under the clear moonlight. The great stretches of wild green looked calm and cool in the quiet of the starry night. They gave a sigh of content, and began their usual walk, arm in arm. Up the West Heath Road to the Pond, to the left along the Spaniards Road. They drank in the clear, crisp air appreciatively. "You're such a *lamb*," said Essie, with a loving pressure on his arm. "Just so you don't think I'm perfect, when I'm not," he said, returning the pressure. "Oh, I think you're much nicer than perfect," she said. Then, returning to her old habit of everlasting discussion, for she had learned that by discussion they came nearer to perfect understanding, she said: "Now, if you really wanted to trot out your faults, you

153

should have mentioned your great original sin."
"Which is?" "Laziness, with a capital L," she replied emphatically. "It's the cause of most of your shortcomings." Paul was interested, because he was convinced, in spite of all he said, that Essie knew and understood him better than anyone else. "Take your disloyalty to your friends, which is so hard for me to excuse. It's really laziness. When you're away from them, and you usually are, you're actually too lazy to send them a card or write them a letter, though you know how much pleasure it would give them to hear from you. And would you seriously go out of your way to prove to them that you love them? Not you—you're too lazy." "But they understand," he protested feebly. "Huh, they spoil you, like I do. Take your work. You never learn the lines of your plays until the last moment, when you simply are ashamed to read them any longer. Just think, perhaps if you learned your lines first, then thought about them during rehearsals, and could give your whole attention to direction and action, you might be able to get so much more out of plays than you do. I'm not saying that you don't do very well," she said hastily, "but you might do even better. Take your concerts, for instance; you just won't learn a new song until

you're convinced that you can't sing the same old programme any longer. And really, darling"— very seriously—"I think that's half the reason for your feeling about singing other music. You realise that you will have to get down to brass tacks and study, learn how to sing them correctly, learn the languages so you can articulate the words clearly and easily, read about the composers, their lives and their countries, so you can understand the spirit of the songs. I know you wouldn't sing them unless you could sing them intelligently and understandingly. So what do you do? You're too lazy to dig in and work, so you settle back and say, 'I'm a special interpreter of the Music of My People,' and stop there, because you know *that* music, its full meaning, its background, its whole significance, and no work is required for you to sing it really well. Take *Othello*. You're fond of saying, 'I think I'll wait till I've had more experience in the theatre before I undertake that; it requires maturity.' When what you really mean is, 'I've got to learn how to speak the English language properly before I can undertake that play. I'll have to learn the rôle, learn how to walk in strange clothes, learn to talk in a strange idiom; I'll have to read a great deal about Shakespeare, his time, his works

155

themselves, before I can fully understand the play.' Oh, I admit when you do a thing you do it intelligently, thoroughly, magnificently. But my point is that you don't do it till you're run down and must. And it's all because you're so everlastingly lazy." Essie was seething with ambition for him, with a great pride in his ability. They sat down in the moonlight, and Paul instinctively reached in his pocket for the coppers to pay for their seats. He was tremendously interested. "Do you really think I could play Othello now, if I worked at it?" he asked thoughtfully. "I know you can, silly." "All right, I'll do it. I'll tell Maurice Browne so the next time he asks me," he said with determination. "Attaboy," shouted Essie enthusiastically, placing a resounding kiss on his cheek. They sat with their arms about each other, planning. "And I'll have a go at those German songs too. Larry is always after me to try some over. I do the arias from 'The Magic Flute' now, and 'The Two Grenadiers,' but not well enough to include them on my programmes," he said doubtfully. "That's because you haven't really studied them and thought about them, and worked over them seriously," said Essie promptly; "you could do them magnificently." "All right, I'll try them." They sat there a little

156

LONDON'S CRITICS ACCLAIM ROBESON

They Check Verdict of First Nighters on "Othello"

"HAILED AS GREAT ARTIST"

Question of Color Frankly Discussed and Dismissed

From The World's Bureau

LONDON, May 30.—Eight out of twelve London dramatic critics to-day proclaimed Paul Robeson's first performance of Othello here last night as a magnificent and outstanding achievement—a verdict that has turned last evening's premiere into one of the milestones in recent English theatrical history.

The occasion is uniquely marked by an editorial in to-day's Morning Post—high priestess of die-hard Tory exclusiveness and culture—which said in part: "Last night Mr. Paul Robeson played Othello, and the occasion was one of considerable artistic interest. The interest, however, was due not to the fact that Mr. Robeson is a man of color and that Shakespeare gave to Othello many characteristics that belong rather to the Negro than to the Moor, but to the fact that Mr. Robeson is a very great artist. His success both as singer and actor has been remarkable and the interest lay in some further discovery of the range of his remarkable talents."

White and Black

Robeson even pleased the hypercritical Hannen Swaffer of the Daily Express. He said "Paul Robeson destroyed last night the foolish idea accepted for many years that Iago is a better part than Othello. Robeson's art conquered everything. 'Why should a black actor be allowed to kiss a white actress?', I heard a few people say beforehand. There was no protest of that kind in the theatre. 'Twas in the part and that was that. When his rage came it was magnificent."

This review is typical of those of most other critics. Ivor Brown, distinguished critic of the Manchester Guardian and the Sunday Observer, ended his eulogistic review with the words, "As far as the male side of the cast was concerned this Othello was a one man band; but Mr. Robeson's music, with all its majesty of tone and sweep of power, does not make that form of orchestra tremendous."

The Daily Telegraph said: "Much debate of the question as to whether Shakespeare meant Othello to be a Negro or an Arab can be left to the professors; but it is certainly true that by reason of his race Mr. Robeson was able to surmount difficulties which English actors generally find in the part of Othello without even seeming to notice that they are there."

Robeson Was Nervous

Robeson, in an interview here this afternoon, after reading of his success, admitted the nervousness he felt on the first night.

"They seem pleased about me and I'm surprised," he said, "for I was nervous last night and I started off with my performance pitched a bit higher than I wanted it to be."

The color question is frankly met by Miss Peggy Aschroft, last night's Desdemona. She said this afternoon: "It never occurred to me. Racial prejudices are foolish at the best of times; but I think it is positively absurd that they should even come into consideration where acting is concerned.

"I suppose Mr. Robeson kissed me during the play about five times. Ever so many people asked me if I didn't mind, and it seemed so silly. Of course I didn't mind. I see no difference in being kissed by Paul Robeson and being kissed by any other actor. It's just necessary to the play. For myself I look on it as a real privilege to act with a great artist like Paul Robeson."

longer, quiet and happy, breathing in the clear, fresh air and thinking eagerly about his work and the bright future. Later, many of their problems were discussed and threshed out on those seats along the Spaniards Road in the quiet early morning hours. They liked to take a turn along the Heath before they went to bed, no matter what the hour.

One morning when the Robesons were breakfasting in their home in Hampstead, their small son, Paul, junior, came in. Mrs. Goode, his grandmother, beamed. She secretly thought Paul saw far too little of his baby, and that he was strangely lacking in interest in the child. "Ah," she said, pleased at finding them, "good morning, son. And here is *your* son." She turned to the baby, a small, brown, sturdy, adorable rascal, ridiculously like his father. "Say good morning to Daddy." Large Paul looked bored and tried to conceal his irritation. Small Paul did not even hear his grandmother; he was gazing at the table with eager eyes. "Cweam, suyar, coffee," he said, and let go the full charm of his smile, dimples, and baby teeth upon his mother, hoping she would allow him to put lumps of sugar carefully into her cup, and guide his fat hand while he poured in the cream. Paul was interested in his son's increasing vocabulary. But Mrs. Goode was not content. "Paul," she said, with an attempt at severity, "say good morning to Daddy; shake hands with Daddy." The baby, arrested by the tone of her voice, dragged his fascinated gaze away from the cups on the table, hastily went up to his father, and said, without interest, "Goo' mornin', Daddy," shook hands solemnly, and then rushed back to his mother's knee, imploring her with his eyes for the coveted privilege. Essie was uncomfortable, realising how extremely annoyed her husband was with her mother. She did her best to distract his attention by showing the child off to best advantage. Climbing up on her lap, he reached for the sugar and placed two lumps in her cup; then he poured the cream in; as Essie poured the coffee he leaned far out of the way of the steam; his eyes were shining with interest and pleasure; he leaned forward to "shtir" it, then sat back happily and said: "Dwink." Now thoroughly content, he climbed down from her knee and began to play about the room. Essie, her mother, and Paul chatted about the affairs of the day. The baby, playing under the table, became entangled with his father's legs; following one out and patting it affectionately, he

158

emerged and looked up with an adorable friendly smile: "Daddy's laig. Ha-o, Daddy dear." His father returned his smile and pat with an affectionate "Hello, Paul," and the child continued playing. "Wasn't that sweet?" said Mrs. Goode. Paul looked at her for a long moment, then said very seriously: "Tell me, Mother, did you get the significance of that? It's very important to me, and I just want you to understand how I feel about the boy and his training. I really don't care if he isn't taught 'manners' in the usual sense at all. They don't mean anything. Just let him alone; he's a nice boy; he'll speak to people when he wants to. I think it's terrible to make the poor little chap go the rounds and say good morning to everybody, simply because it's supposed to be the right thing to do. I don't think it's the right thing; I don't do it myself. I only say good morning if I feel like it. Take this morning. You made him be polite to me. He said good morning dutifully, but he didn't even see me or realise I was in the room until he discovered my 'laig' just now. So his greeting meant nothing to him nor to me. But when *he* found me, and *wanted* to say good morning, he did it in his own charming way." "Yes, I see what you mean," said his mother-in-law thoughtfully. "But you know he will live in a conventional world, and I thought good manners would help him to get on in it." "The devil with good manners," answered Paul heatedly. "If he's a nice, friendly, intelligent child he'll instinctively have good manners. As a matter of fact," he continued seriously, "the less he's taught the better I'll be pleased. The poor little fellow has enough to learn, anyway, without being taught a lot of unimportant stuff. It would please me enormously if you and Essie would arrange for him to have at least two hours a day absolutely alone, so he can play by himself and use his own little imagination and develop it. Two hours with just someone to keep an eye on him, but not to talk to him, play with him, nor pay any attention whatever to him. I feel that that will be of great importance to his development. If you'll arrange that I'll be pleased." Essie and her mother exchanged glances; they were delighted with this interest in the baby. "Why, of course," said Mrs. Goode, interested. "I think you're right. He will use his own little mind and think up things for himself." She had undertaken the task of bringing up the child with a deep and loving sense of responsibility. She knew that Essie and Paul had every confidence in her sound intelligence and

160

good sense, and that made her all the more anxious to listen to all suggestions, and to make no mistakes. She looked at Paul with anxious interest; he caught her look and smiled back. "Of course, he's Essie's child, and she's to do whatever she likes with him. She had him against my judgment, and went through hell for him, so she has every right to do with him as she thinks fit. Only you both are always so anxious to have him like me, and me him, and he seems such a dear little fellow, that I hate to see him forced in any way. I'd like him to have the things I missed. If I had had some time in my childhood that wasn't blocked out and filled in for me, I think my imagination would have been more developed. As it is I've almost none. All my time was crowded with lessons to learn, games to play, books to read. I never can remember having had hours in which I had nothing to do, and had actually to entertain myself out of my own mind. I'd like him to have that." "He certainly shall." Mrs. Goode took her grandson to the nursery for his lunch. As he left the dining-room he chuckled delightedly: "Pwunes, Daddy dear; goo' bye," and, bestowing his wide grin upon his parents, he trotted happily away. He adored his prunes.

161

Paul felt like talking. "You know, darling, I don't want you to be disappointed in my lack of interest in the boy. He's a nice baby. But I have no fatherly instinct about him at all. What he needs now is food and sleep and air and exercise, and intelligent letting-alone. When he's older and we can talk, I'm sure I'll be more interested. But now I'm busy with my work and he has people to look after him, so why try to force me to take up a lot of time with him? After a while, when I have more time and he's old enough to be interesting, I'm sure we'll have great times together. Meanwhile he's just a cute, charming baby." "All right dear," answered his wife. "We'll try not to force him on you." Then she added dreamily, "He's ridiculously like you; the likeness is positively uncanny." "Which makes it all exactly as you wished," he said, kissing her affectionately. "Oh, and one thing more about the boy. If we settle permanently here in England as we hope to, I particularly want him to go to America at regular intervals, so he will know his own people. And it would be grand to take him to Africa. I want him to have *roots*. I want him to know Negroes. I feel it will be very important for him." "Yes, it will be," agreed Essie. "If he's to be an artist in any sense of the

162

word, his racial contacts will be of great value to
him. It's great fun to see how he likes coloured
people already. He's crazy about one of the teachers at his morning nursery school, simply because
she's dark; she looks like an Italian. He calls her
'Martin,' and talks about her a great deal. And
when people come in for tea, he will always pass
by the white people and make straight for the
coloured person. 'Brown,' he will say with the
sweetest, most affectionate, eager expression. I
think he must feel that we, the people he knows
and loves best, are brown, and that the brown skin
in itself is a mark of kinship." "That's great. I
don't want him to be prejudiced. I want him to
know and feel that he is a Negro."

They went up to the drawing-room arm in arm.
Paul sprawled into a huge easy chair, sitting on
the end of his spine, his long legs draped over the
arm of the chair. "The springs of that chair won't
last much longer," Essie thought with annoyance,
as she sank down on the divan. She had never been
able to outgrow her disapproval of her husband's
habit of sprawling. "Why can't he sit in a chair
properly?" she thought impatiently; she had long
ago ceased protesting to him about it. Paul smiled
at her through his cigarette smoke. His face looked

full of good news. "I feel like working," he said. "I stopped in at Bumpus's yesterday and got a lot of books I wanted"; his eyes danced mischievously. "You'll faint when you get the bill; it's about eight pounds." "Good heavens, what on earth did you buy?" "All of Shakespeare's plays, several critical books on him, a swell pocket edition of *Othello*, that new book on Moussorgsky, that two-volume book on Bach, the book of translations of the Schubert songs, the life of Schubert, a marvellous book on Beethoven —— And the Gramophone Company is sending me Beethoven's Concerto in D Major with Kreisler and the Berlin State Opera Orchestra playing, the César Franck Symphony, the Schubert Trio in B Flat Major, and a lot more grand records. Very decent of them, isn't it?" "That means you're going to begin on *Othello* and on the German songs," said Essie, pleased at the thoroughness with which he was going about it. Paul stretched his long arms above his head and grinned. "Yes, I feel the urge. I feel I could work a year. I'm really interested this time." "I'm so glad; I'll help." Days, weeks, months slipped by with Paul spending long hours shut up with his gramophone, playing the fine records over and over, soaking himself in good music; reading his

164

books, buying new books and devouring them; working with Larry, learning songs. He bought a metronome. "That easy rhythm of Negro music has made me careless of the value of notes," he said. He worked hard with his teachers over the new songs. He read *Othello*, and actually learned his lines more than seven months before he was contracted to report for rehearsal. Essie was impressed, deeply respectful, and happy. Paul was happy in his work. "When I do *Othello* they'll all expect a crusted American accent. I'll fool 'em. I'll do the rôle in good honest English, as pure as I can make it, because pure English will bring out the music of the text. Why, I might as well sing the Negro dialect of the spirituals with a correct Boston accent, as do *Othello* in 'American.' " He was like a small boy in his enthusiasm and intense activity.

"Oh-ho! young man," said Larry, meeting the Robeson baby one day at the door of the Hampstead house. "Ha-o, Warry," answered young Paul, dimpling. "Take my hand and we'll go in together," said Larry, pleased that the child knew his name. The baby solemnly led him straight into the library and up to the piano. "Moosik," said he. Larry laughed delightedly. "The boy has brains," he said. Essie and Paul came in, Essie

165

full of the trip they were starting on next day. They were going on their first concert tour of Central Europe, and all three were thrilled. "We'll pick you up at eleven o'clock in the taxi," Essie told Larry as she left the two men to rehearse, "the boat-train leaves Victoria at eleven-thirty." "You know I'll be ready." Larry was always ready and on hand fifteen minutes before he was due. The Robesons were always late, and just made trains by fractions of a minute in great excitement; they had been known to miss trains. They all arrived at Victoria at eleven-twenty the following morning, Essie carrying the tickets and the itinerary as usual. As she directed the porters she told the representative from the travel bureau that they were taking the eleven-thirty boat-train for the Dover-Ostend crossing to catch the Brussels express to Vienna. "Oh, you've missed that connection," the official told her calmly, "it was ten-thirty, not eleven-thirty." "Oh, no," insisted Essie, sure of her ground, "see I have it here from your office— eleven-thirty." "Well, the office made a mistake," he answered as he reached for the tickets and itinerary. Paul and Larry stood aside, looking very much as though they wanted to giggle. This made Essie furious. She went off with the official to the

166

"THE EMPEROR JONES"

Photo: Joan Craven

ticket office, and found that there was a mistake in her schedule, and that the train by which they were to make all their connections had been gone an hour. She was deeply chagrined; she scolded the official in no uncertain terms. New tickets had to be bought, wires sent to Brussels. They crowded into the eleven-thirty Dover-Calais train just as it was pulling out of the station. Essie was so angry she was helpless. Paul and Larry were almost hysterical with laughter. "How dared they make that mistake," she thundered. Larry could hold in no longer. "There she was, bustling about and herding us and the luggage so efficiently," he exploded between bursts of merriment. "What tickles me so is the fact that she's mad because it's a reflection on her efficiency and her dignity as a manager—not because we missed our connections and our sleepers and may be late for the Vienna concert," said Paul, wiping the tears of laughter from his eyes. "How dared they," raged Essie, furious. But soon they had laughed her out of her ill-humour, and she was rejoicing with them over the shorter Channel crossing. The whole trip became an adventure; she just managed to find the sleepers, to catch the important trains. Both men teased her unmercifully, and she had to laugh with them at herself.

167

In Vienna, Prague, and Budapest they had new triumphs. Everywhere they had crowded, enthusiastic houses, and everywhere critics wrote rhapsodic reviews of Paul's voice, his personality, and the music. Hungarians, Austrians, Czechs, proudly entertained him; American ambassadors attended his concerts, congratulated him, and entertained in his honour. Paul was especially proud of this great compliment, for many reasons. This is what the Viennese critic, Siegfried Geyer, wrote about him in *Die Stunde* of April 11th, 1929:

"The public, scenting a sensation, filled the hall, as it has not been filled for a long time. The public always scents something, even if it is not the right thing. People wanted to see a Negro—they wanted to see how a Negro sings; and they suddenly found themselves assisting at an important artistic event. The cheap popular sensation did not materialise; what did materialise was a sensation of a different order. This magnificently built Negro in evening clothes, with his glistening white shirt-front— Africa in European evening-dress—is a phenomenon among singers, a marvel in his power of expressing the innermost feelings; you sit spellbound and stunned by the magic of such a performance.

168

"For several days there has been some very loud beating of the Negro drum. We were distrustful, as always in the case of such vigorous publicity. But a real artist was before us. We realised that there was truth behind the announcements that he was to play 'Emperor Jones' under the direction of Max Reinhardt. Assuredly he is an actor who can give dramatic form to the primeval elements of his race —who embodies the hunted feeling of a tortured creature, the tragedy of the coloured man in the midst of a white society which credits itself with a character corresponding to the colour of its skin. When the man began to sing one of those negro spirituals filled with the deepest melancholy— when, slow and full, came the first words, 'Wade in the Water'—the hall suddenly grew hushed and still; we were listening to organ-tones of a purity seldom heard. And what followed—one spiritual after another—confirmed the phenomenon which the Negro singer represents—a voice which is no mere function of the larynx, but of which the motive-force is the soul.

"In 'Water Boy,' a genuine folk-song, with an almost joyous background, Robeson revealed more of the true personality of his race than half a dozen learned writings and discourses. 'I don't feel no

ways tired' was the crowning achievement of the
man's creative fancy—a tempestuous climax in the
prophetic words which foretell happier days to
come and wing their way to a heavenly city with
jubilant Hallelujahs; a hymn to a new and freer
outlook on the world, to which Paul Robeson's
deep notes do homage.

"A wonderful evening, such as comes only once
or twice a year. It was not a matter of top notes;
there was no registering of the high F; it is of no
interest to anyone how high his register reaches. It
embraces all that is human in a human being. That
is enough. Vienna realised it at once. There was a
storm of jubilant applause. The audience stamped
and shouted. The wild men were in the stalls; on
the stage stood a modest Negro."

There is something about Paul Robeson that
inspires enthusiasm which can only be expressed
in superlatives. People who know him or have
heard him invariably use terms such as wonderful,
marvellous, great artist, great man. He has a quality of greatness that comes through whatever he
does. From his high school days, people have said
and written that he was a remarkable student, one
of the greatest athletes of his time, a magnificent

actor. In America, in England, on the Continent, people feel and appreciate that quality of greatness. He is always glad and proud when he wins new laurels, but he remains modest, simple, lovable.

And now, when he strolls down the main streets of the large cities of the world, people recognise him. His handsome, almost Grecian figure and his dark-brown African face cannot easily be mistaken. People stare and whisper excitedly, "That's Paul Robeson." If they know him they rush up to greet him, sure of the wide, welcoming grin. He has friends everywhere. He leaves a trail of friendliness wherever he goes, this Paul Robeson, Negro, who, with his typically Negro qualities—his appearance, his voice, his genial smile, his laziness, his child-like simplicity—is carving his place as a citizen of the world, a place which would most certainly have made his slave father proud.

APPENDIX. PAUL ROBESON AS AN ATHLETE

New York Sunday Tribune, November 25th, 1917:

RUTGERS BLANKS NAVY

*Dashing Robeson Humbles Black's Noted
Warriors Vaunted Power of Widely
Heralded Newport Naval Reserves
Fades Before Attack of Sanford's Team,
Led by Tall Negro Youth*

Rutgers Win 14—0

By Louis Lee Arms

A tall, tapering Negro in a faded crimson sweater, moleskins, and a pair of maroon socks ranged hither and yon on a wind-whipped Flatbush field yesterday afternoon. He rode on the wings of the frigid breezes; a grim, silent, and compelling figure. Whether it was Charley Barrett, of old Cornell and All-American glory, or Gerrish or

Gardner who tried to hurl himself through a moiling gauntlet he was met and stopped by this blaze of red and black.

The Negro was Paul Robeson, of Rutgers College, and he is a minister's son. He is also nineteen years of age and weighs two hundred pounds. Of his football capacity you are duly referred to "Cupid" Black of Newport and Yale. He can tell you. It was Robeson, a veritable Othello of battle, who led the dashing little Rutgers eleven to a 14–0 victory over the widely heralded Newport Naval Reserves.

Veterans in football experience, versed in its fantastic and multiform arts, and popularly designated as the strongest football eleven in the United States, the thick-set Naval warriors came down from Newport upon victory and added glory bent. They had trimmed Brown and Harvard, and that the smooth-skinned youths from the banks of the Raritan could stop them—well, it was beyond belief.

But it wasn't. The Navy's last transitory show of impressiveness faded when their signal practice was done and the referee's whistle blew on the opening quarter. For forty-four minutes thereafter

Foster Sanford's ghost-footed machine ran the Navy's ends and pierced her bulking line, and, in other words, gave Dr. Bull, "Cupid" Black, *et al.*, as pretty a drubbing as you please.

The Navy was perplexed and then stung by this amazing actuality; then it was enveloped completely in the tracery of Rutgers' perfected attack, and it fought blindly and wrathfully to stave off a lopsided defeat.

As a thorn in her flesh the tall, tapering Robeson, commanding Rutgers' secondary, dived under and spilled her wide, oblique angled runs, turned back her line plunges, and carried the burden of the defence so splendidly that in forty-four minutes these ex-All-American backs, who are fixed luminaries in the mythology of the gridiron, made precisely two first downs. . . .

Among the original tactical manœuvres in Rutgers' attack is the calling in of Robeson to open holes for the back field. He is shifted by signal from left end to whatever spot along the line had been pre-selected. Thus considerable of Rutgers' line drives were put upon the basis of Robeson's superiority over Black, Schlacter, Callahan, or whomever he faced.

174

PAUL ROBESON, NEGRO

New York Tribune, October 28th, 1917:

RUTGERS BLANKS FORDHAM

*Robeson, Giant Negro, Plays Leading Rôle For
Jersey Eleven*

By Charles A. Taylor

A dark cloud upset the hopes of the Fordham
eleven yesterday afternoon. Its name was Robeson,
and it travelled all the way across the Jersey
meadows from the banks of the old Raritan to the
Bronx. There was no semblance of a silver lining
to this cloud, and the maroon football warriors
were completely smothered by it and its accom-
panying galaxy of Rutgers' stars. The score was
28–0 in favour of the dark cloud.

Robeson, the giant Negro, appeared in the
line-up as left end, but he did not confine himself
to this particular post. He played in turn practically every position in the Rutgers team before
the battle was ended.

With his team on the offensive, Robeson was
wont to leap high in the air to grab forward passes
wherever he saw that a man they were intended for
was in another sector of the battle field. On the

175

defence he was kept busy on the few occasions when Fordham appeared likely to make a score.

Robeson was supposed to play full-back on the defensive, and he did, but never did a full-back range so widely as he. If there was a gap in the line Robeson filled it. If the Rutgers ends were the least bit remiss in stopping the dashes of Erwig and Frisch, Robeson was on hand to prevent any substantial progress.

The dark cloud was omnipresent, but he had valuable assistance in his team-mates. . . . It would be wrong to say that Robeson is the entire Rutgers team. The aggregation is too well balanced for that, but it was this dark cloud that cut off all the sunshine for the Fordham rooters yesterday.

New York World, November 28th, 1917:

ROBESON TAKES A PLACE
WITH ELECT OF FOOTBALL

All Around Ability of Rutgers' End Puts Him with Greatest and Best of the Game

By George Daley

Paul Robeson, the big Negro end of the Rutgers eleven, is a football genius. Two or three weeks ago George Foster Sanford, speaking with conviction born of long experience in the game, said:

"Robeson is the best all-around player on the gridiron this season and the most valuable to the team."

After seeing his play at Ebbett's Field on Saturday against "Cupid" Black's Naval Reserve team the disposition is to go Sanford one better and say that Robeson must be ranked with such men as Tack Hardwick and Eddie Mahan of Harvard, Charley Barrett of Cornell, Jim Thorpe of the Carlisle Indians, Elmer Oliphant of West Point, and Ted Coy of Yale for all-around ability in football.

It is seldom indeed that a linesman can develop such versatility. Robeson does about everything except carry the ball, and everything he does may be marked "sterling." It seems a pity that Sanford did not go a step further, and out of the many duties assigned to Robeson add one which would give him the ball for a running play.

It is quite possible that such a play is or was included in his wide repertoire, but that the need for it did not arise on Saturday. In any case, here are some of the duties imposed on this super-man of the game:

Opening up holes for his backs on line plays; providing remarkable interference for his backs on end runs; going down the field under punts; taking

177

forward passes, in which, by the way, he handles the pigskin with almost the same sureness as a baseball; supporting the centre of the line on defence, or, as some have it, playing "defensive quarterback"; plugging up holes from one end of the line to the other; tackling here, there, and everywhere; kicking off and diagnosing.

And the greatest perhaps of his accomplishments is accurate diagnosing. His ability to size up plays and quickly get to the point of danger is almost uncanny. He is so rarely at fault that he is at the centre of practically every play, and therein lies his greatest value, and therein is the truest measure of his all-around ability.